MW01687991

PHILLIP E. MAHFOOD

CUSTOMER CRISIS

TURNING AN UNHAPPY CUSTOMER INTO A LIFE-LONG CLIENT

PROBUS PUBLISHING COMPANY
Chicago, Illinois
Cambridge, England

© 1993, Phillip E. Mahfood

ALL RIGHTS RESERVED. No part of this publication may be reproduced, stored in a retrieval system, or transmitted, in any form or by any means, electronic, mechanical, photocopying, recording, or otherwise, without the prior written permission of the publisher and the copyright holder.

This publication is designed to provide accurate and authoritative information in regard to the subject matter covered. It is sold with the understanding that the author and the publisher are not engaged in rendering legal, accounting, or other professional service.

Authorization to photocopy items for internal or personal use, or the internal or personal use of specific clients, is granted by PROBUS PUBLISHING COMPANY, provided that the U.S. $7.00 per page fee is paid directly to Copyright Clearance Center, 27 Congress Street, Salem, MA 01970, USA; Phone: 1-508-744-3350. For those organizations that have been granted a photocopy license by CCC, a separate system of payment has been arranged. The fee code for users of the Transactional Reporting Service is 1-55738-421-5/93/$00.00 + $7.00.

ISBN 1-55738-421-5

Printed in the United States of America

BB

1 2 3 4 5 6 7 8 9 0

CB

Probus books are available at quantity discounts when purchased for business, educational, or sales promotional use. For more information, please call the Director, Corporate / Institutional Sales at (800) 998-4644, or write:

Director, Corporate / Institutional Sales
Probus Publishing Company
1925 N. Clybourn Avenue
Chicago, IL 60614
***PHONE* (800) 998-4644 *FAX* (312) 868-6250**

Dedication

This book is dedicated to Karen.
She is more than my wife, my comforter, and my strength.
She's also my best friend.

Table of Contents

Preface ix

Acknowledgments xiii

Introduction xv

Exhibit A xvi
Word-of-Mouth Advertising xvii
Preventive Maintenance xix

Chapter One
Satisfied Customers Are Not an Accident 1

Customer/Merchant Relationship 3
Perceived Value 5
Customer Killers 7
Rewarding Excellence 9

Chapter Two
The Importance of Procedure 13

Spreading the Pain 14
Establish Channels of Authority 18

Developing the Proper Paperwork 20
Historic Perspective of the Product 20
Product Complaint Survey 22
Historic Charting of a Specific Customer's Complaint Activity . . . 23
Accurate Verification and Identification of Defective Products and Services 24
Customer Complaint Survey 25
Establishing a Customer Resolution Area 27

Chapter Three
Determine the Minimum Requirement to Solve the Crisis 31

Performing Triage in the Complaint Department 37
Analyze Minimum Action Required to Resolve the Crisis 39
The Nature of the Problem 41
The Nature of the Product 42
The Nature of the Customer 43
The Nature of the Store 43
Determining a Proper Course of Action 44
Does a Problem Really Exist? 44

Chapter Four
Can the Customer Be Satisfied? 47

Act with Dispatch 48
Offer a Satisfactory Resolution 50
What to Do If an Offer Is Refused 52

Chapter Five
Determining the Origin of the Problem 55

Advertising as the Culprit 55
Customer Education 57

Educating the Staff 61
Vender Cooperation in Quality Control 66

Chapter Six
Writing Resolution Reports: The Need for Complete and Accurate Records 69

Strength of a Written Report versus a Verbal Report 70
Reinforcement of Company Policy 71
Reports as Training Tools 72
Establishing a Livable Procedure 73
Procedures in Relation to Industry Standards 73
Procedures in Relation to Regional Expectations 75
Procedures in Relation to Vendors 76
Procedures in Relation to Customer Expectations 79

Chapter Seven
Answering the Bell 81

Establishing Telephone Policies 84
How to Answer 84
The Urgency of Proper Training 87
The Mechanics of Handling Incoming Calls 89
Urgency of the Call 89
The Expectation of the Caller 90
Telephone Problem Resolution 91
Being a Messenger 94
Time and Date 95
Who Called? 96
The Crux of the Call 97
Action! 99
Screening Incoming Calls 101
The Invisible Screen 101
Prioritize the Call 102

Qualify the Caller 106
Protection for the Called 108

Chapter Eight
Handling Letters of Complaint 113

The Mailman Cometh 114
The Little Complaint 115
The Medium Complaint 120
The Massive Complaint 123

Chapter Nine
Pulling It All Together 127

Learning to Listen 127
Body Language 129
Finding an Opening 130
Looking, Acting, and Being Concerned 131
Accepting Responsibility 132
Avoid One-Word Answers 133
Action versus Reaction 134

Epilogue 137

Appendix Schedule

Appendix A	Stansell Communications	141
Appendix B	Berg-Moran Construction	149
Appendix C	Danka Business Systems	153
Appendix D	J C Penney Company, Inc.	159
Appendix E	Six Flags Over Texas	161
Appendix F	Wilson Trading Company	167

Index 171

Preface

A few years ago I was in a department store about to purchase a major electronic component system. I had many major obstacles to overcome before I would be allowed to make a several thousand dollar purchase. I would first need to find a sales clerk, explain what I needed, point out the system that would suit my needs, and then convince the hapless store employee to take my money and ring up the sale.

I know this sounds ridiculous, but I assure you, that's how I felt. It was almost as if the store was working against making me a customer. But the problems I had finding someone to sell me the unit I wanted were nothing compared to the lack of follow-up service I encountered. I realized, when telling my close circle of about 50 people about the horrible experience I'd had, that they too were filled with war stories of their own of dealing with the horrors of a service-starved America.

My employees, I reasoned, were as customer oriented as they were because I had trained them myself. But what about other companies? How did stores expect to turn a profit if they treated all their customers as badly as I had been treated? I wasn't writing business books then: I was busily engaged in the actual day-to-day battle of winning the commerce war. Then one day the unthinkable happened. I received a letter from one of my oldest customers. He informed me that because of sloppy service, he was taking his business elsewhere.

I was livid! Heads would roll; people would be packing their belongings into cardboard boxes before the day was over. I summoned my operations manager and showed him the letter. How could this have happened? How could our staff have been so lax as to allow a customer of this size to simply slip away? His answer? I hadn't told him that service was that big a deal with me, and he in turn hadn't stressed it with our staff. After all, he reasoned, we hire only the best people, mostly college graduates, and surely they already knew the basics of customer service.

He was right. It wasn't his fault, or any other employee in my company. The fault lay with my own lack of leadership. But from that day to this, the one aspect of our company that remains absolutely firm is our dedication to giving the best service we can possibly provide. I wrote this book not because we don't all know what we should do, but rather because we sometimes fail to pass what we know on to the people who work for us and with us.

Look at any new business. It doesn't matter if it's a law office or a new automobile manufacturer, the one consistent value found in each new venture is the realization that to do better than their competition they must provide better service than is now available in the marketplace. Young companies know this; old companies forget this. Many factors change as a business matures: policies become buried under new policies, layers of bureaucracy cover over the spirit of entrepreneurship, and we find ourselves bloated with rules and procedures.

If any company hopes to maintain the competitive edge it once had, and can have again, it must dedicate itself to the concept that it is easier to keep a customer than to make a new one. I've been in business since I was 10 years old. I know what I have to do to keep my business growing. And so do you: fulfill a need. It's just that simple. But along with that basic tenet is the unwritten law of business: provide your customers with service that'll make him or her want to tell the spouse about it over supper that night, and you'll have an edge on your competitors that will drive them to rack and ruin.

Chapters 1 through 9 deal with the mechanics of establishing and controlling a customer problem resolution center. The Appendix presents case studies of how other companies have dealt with the question of customer service. As you read this book, remember two things. First, no two companies are exactly alike. What works for one may not exactly work for another. You must take from this book what is reasonable for you and your company and modify it to work for you. Second, all companies are exactly alike! In the final analysis, what works for General Motors and Pop's Lemonade Stand will work for you, too. There are many formulas for successful management of any business, but no formula will work—*not one*—that doesn't include customer service as its foundation.

Phillip E. Mahfood

Acknowledgments

I gratefully acknowledge the help and assistance of the following people, without whose help I doubt seriously I'd have ever finished this book:

Richard K. Blaine
Kevin Hoffman
Mike L. Lowe
Duncan Muir
Bruce Neal
Jim Stansell
Pamela van Giessen
Janette Walsh

Introduction

There is only one customer more detrimental to your company's well being than the one who is unsatisfied and complains; the one who is unsatisfied and doesn't complain. The customer who complains is giving your company a chance to make amends, to make good on its promises to satisfy all buyers. The customer who doesn't tell you about his unhappy relations with your company is the one who simply leaves your store and never comes back. Can you afford him? Look at the chart on the next page.

If a business only loses one customer a day, and each of those customers was spending five dollars per week, the total loss of revenue is $94,900.00 annually. Five dollars a week is not a great deal of money, but the aggregate amount is staggering. What if the business is a grocery store that loses two customers a day because of poor service? It is not inconceivable that the

Potential Annual Revenue Loss

Customer Dollars Spent per Week	Number of Customers Lost per Day						
	1	2	5	10	20	50	100
$5	$ 94,900	$ 189,800	$ 474,500	$ 949,000	$ 1,898,000	$ 4,745,000	$ 9,940,000
$10	189,800	379,600	949,000	1,898,000	3,796,000	9,490,000	18,980,000
$50	949,000	1,898,000	4,745,000	9,490,000	18,980,000	47,450,000	94,900,000
$100	1,898,000	3,796,000	9,490,000	18,980,000	37,960,000	94,900,000	189,800,000
$200	3,796,000	7,592,000	18,980,000	37,960,000	75,920,000	189,800,000	379,600,000
$300	5,694,000	11,388,000	28,470,000	56,940,000	113,880,000	284,700,000	569,400,000

Source: Customer Service Institute, 1010 Wayne Avenue, Silver Spring, MD 20910, (301) 585-0730.

store would lose an average of fifty dollars per week for each customer they lose. The gross loss over a period of one year is almost $2,000,000.00!

American business spends a king's ransom every year in advertising. Costs of advertising are figured in units of shares of an audience. This is to say that the number of customers who visit a store as the direct result of the store's advertising efforts is divided into the cost of that advertising to arrive at a figure of cost per customer. This cost per customer is a factor which allows companies to evaluate the cost effectiveness of their advertising programs. A newspaper ad which cost $750 and resulted in 60 people coming into the store has a cost factor of twelve dollars and fifty cents per customer. In other words, it cost the company $12.50 for each customer they attracted with their ad. Had only 30 people responded to the ad, the cost would have been $25.00 per share.

It is possible to calculate what a business pays per customer by dividing their advertising budget by the number of customers who walk into their store each year. Of course, the cost of advertising is figured into the price of the goods or services. Like other operating expenses, advertising is calculated to induce and expand the number of dollars customers spend with the business. But there is another form of advertising that is absolutely free. It's called "word-of-mouth," and it comes in two forms, positive and negative.

Word-of-Mouth Advertising

Word-of-mouth advertising is the original advertising medium, but it relies heavily on the good will of others, so to rely on it exclusively is to court disaster. The up side to word-of-mouth advertising is that it is free, it is credible, and it usually carries no hidden agenda. But the down side is that if a customer is angry with your company, you can be sure he or she will do everything possible to prevent friends and relatives from doing business with your firm. The deep downside is that often you do not even know a problem exists.

Perception is the key to understanding the damage word-of-mouth advertising can do. Consider this scenario: Joe Average stopped at Happy Pantry, purchased a loaf of bread and went home. His wife opened the loaf and made sandwiches. Joe ate his, watched a little television, and went to bed. He got up the next morning, had toast and eggs, and went to work. Do you think he spent a good deal of that morning talking about the great loaf of bread he bought? Now, consider the same story, except that when Joe got home, he opened the loaf and a lizard ran out of the bag, and caused his wife to have a heart attack! What was the subject of conversation the next day?

For the next month of his life, Joe told everyone he met about the lizard-infested bread at Happy Pantry. He couldn't help himself, it's human nature. As Thomas Edison said, "Good news travels by mail, bad news travels by telegraph!" Word-of-mouth can kill a business quicker than any other calamity. Conventional wisdom is that every dissatisfied customer will tell at least twenty-five people about his problems with a particular company. There is no way to stop him from doing it. The only defense your company has is to head off the problem before it becomes unmanageable.

Preventive Maintenance

It has become popular in today's business climate to refer to the cleaning up of a problem as "containment" or "damage control." These are excellent terms to use when referring to customer relations. Without a doubt, even the best-run business will ocassionally run afoul of the dissatisfied customer. Certain events, such as the loss of key employees, or the dropping of an important line, or even merely the perception of an uncaring rep or a non-responsive member of the management team, can result in the unintentional loss of a customer. This is an economic fact of life. But equally true is the fact that in almost every case, something can be done to contain the damage, and if handled right, the dissatisfied customer can become the greatest of allies. Unfortunately for most businesses, this opportunity is often missed.

How can an irate customer become a happy customer? The answer is simple. Make the customer happy. He or she came to your firm with certain expectations. Not the least of these expectations is that the product purchased would perform in a manner consistent with the customer's needs. If it did not, then steps must be taken to bridge the gap that exists between the expectation and the reality. There are six steps which, once in place, will serve as a permanent bridge for most of the problems arising out of customer dissatisfaction. Dissatisfaction is really just another word for disappointment.

When we were kids in school, the authorities would from time to time stage a fire drill. During that drill, we would all exit the building, in an orderly fashion, and assemble in a prearranged location where we would be accounted for. Then, after an assessment of the overall effectiveness of the drill, we would be instructed to return to the classroom. Why did the school disrupt the normal activity of the school day to have us exit the building? Why did they have us exit in an orderly fashion? Why not just holler "FIRE!" and let the students scramble for safety? The answer is that by preparing for the worst scenario, the school was in effect making the best of what might be a disastrous event.

The point of fire drills is to establish a procedure to handle an emergency. And an emergency is any event outside the normal realm of routine. A customer who is unhappy about his or her experience in dealing with your company should clearly be outside the realm of routine. And it's only a disaster if there is no clear-cut procedure for handling the event. It is therefore incumbent upon the company to establish a method for dealing with this event. Not to have a routine established is irresponsible and downright foolhardy. But how does a company go about laying out the escape routes?

The next six chapters of this book will deal with the establishment and execution of the fire drill. We will look at three case studies. The first is of a customer who purchased a set of batteries from an electronics specialty store. The second deals with a customer who purchased a pair of running shoes in a department store. The third is of a customer dissatisfied with the service she received from an extermination company. I've chosen these three examples because they represent a large segment of the general population's dealings with business at large. The rules that will help the electronics store will help almost any type of specialty company, from auto parts dealers to zebra food distributors. They will also be useful to wholesale distributors as well as mail-order catalogs.

The department store scenario will be of use to almost any large retailer, including discount operations, grocery chains, gasoline retailers, and companies that depend on a large volume of gross sales to sustain a decent net profit. I've chosen the exterminator company to represent the services we purchase from companies whose goods are not tangible or "hard," but rather rely on the perception of the customer to ascertain their worth. Firms such as financial institutions, insurance companies, and advertising agencies will profit from these scenarios.

The business of business is to continuously attract customers. While most agree new blood fuels a business, it's equally true that old blood is the oil that keeps it in motion. Old blood is absolutely necessary for continued growth for several reasons. First, an old customer is easier to sell: he or she already knows you and your product. You don't have to reinvent the wheel with each presentation. Secondly, as rapport builds transaction after transaction, and a customer becomes committed to you or your company, the maintenance of that prospect is easier and surer than starting over each time.

An established customer has already demonstrated his ability to generate cash for your company, thereby eliminating the fear that your efforts will result in an aborted transaction due to that customer's inability to provide payment for services or goods. An established customer will often be instrumental in finding new business through word-of-mouth. If he is satisfied in his dealings with your company, the odds are good he'll tell his friends and associates about you. This makes the satisfied customer worth his weight in gold, or at least worth the time you spend keeping him happy.

All too often, however, we tend to regard the "old" customer as a property, a commodity we own. Nothing could be further from the truth! My grandfather used to tell me that in the meat business (his specialty), loyalty is limited to a half-cent a pound. Beyond that, nothing else is certain. If that is a given, and I believe it is, how can we be sure that the service we offer will result in a continued relationship, and more, how can we make that half-cent work for us?

If our customers are indeed as fickle as my grandfather seemed to think they were, then our competitors' customers are equally at risk. To grow a good business, however, requires more than merely the continual exchange of disgruntled customers between vendors. The objective is to attract as many new customers as we can, while retaining the ones we already have through various techniques—such as advertising, entering new markets, and offering new goods—and to end each accounting period better off than we started. While this may seem obvious, it is absolutely amazing how many companies are willing to allow established customers to slip away to the competition, while taking the attitude that there are plenty of fish in the sea!

There is not an unlimited number of fish, nor is the practice of catching fish cheaper than the art of keeping fresh the ones you already have. During the normal course of business, you are going to lose customers. The difference in a successful business, as opposed to one that barely hangs on, is that the former regards his or her customers as assets, while the latter regards them as transient visitors to his or her company's sales room. Unless you are prepared to realize how important your customer base is, and act accordingly to preserve it, you will be destined to continually seek new customers from a widening base of prospects. And that just doesn't make sense.

A business relationship is like a marriage. No union of two people always runs smoothly. Consider this fact: you want your customers to exchange hard currency for a product that is invariably worth less than you are asking. That must be true, or no business would survive. We survive on profit, and that profit is the difference between what a commodity or service costs to produce, and the amount of money received when that commodity or service is sold. Profit is the bottom line in all business transactions. Anyone who tells you otherwise should get out of the business world.

We are in business for one common cause: to make a profit on our goods and time. When we hire an employee, that employee is selling us his time for less than it is worth. His time is his commodity, his talents are his tools. If we paid that employee exactly what his talents are worth at retail, then we would be buying and selling his time for a net profit of zero. He would be earning for us exactly what we are paying him, and he would in effect be negating our purpose in hiring him.

Merchandise works on the same principle. If we sold a product for exactly what we paid for it, we could not make a profit, and in time, we would not have a business. This is a cold reality of life. Now, the good news. Your customer already knows this, and unless he or she's recently fallen off a passing turnip truck, he or she knows you are making a profit on the goods or services you sell. And unless he or she's incredibly short sighted, he or she wants you to make that profit! Only by your making a profit can he or she be assured you will be there to service his or her needs the next time. There is no shame in this, nor is there any reason for a successful business person to feel guilty about making a profit. I have purposely not used the term, "a reasonable profit," because any profit that the traffic bear is reasonable. Profit only becomes unreasonable when it causes a customer to turn elsewhere for his or her needs. When this happens, you have moved beyond the realm of profit into the territory of greed, and greed will never sustain a capitalistic endeavor.

1

Satisfied Customers Are Not an Accident

Ask any person why she or he does business with a particular concern, and the answers you receive will vary from "locale" to "convenience" to "satisfactory service" or "good products." There are as many reasons why a customer spends his dollars where he does as there are customers to spend those dollars. But one fact is overwhelmingly obvious. Few people will continue to spend their money where they are not satisfied with the product or the service. One of the truest aspects of free enterprise is that when we first open our doors, we get very few "free" customers. Granted, there are those businesses, most notably those that enjoy franchise arrangements with municipalities (i.e., power companies, cable television suppliers, telephone companies, etc.), whose operations appear impervious to customer complaints, but even these are subject to the scrutiny of the regulatory agency that oversees their production and public relations.

For the most part, each person who must meet the public in some manner, be it as a salesperson, an installer of a service, a professional, or even a public servant, must to some degree attempt to satisfy the customer whom he or she encounters. Each of us, unless we have somehow found a way to sequester ourselves in a cave and do all our business by fax and modem, must from time to time give consideration to the old saw, "the customer is always right."

But equally true is the fact that no one can please everyone all the time. There are those professional malcontents, those curmudgeons of commerce whose very existence is a bane to reasonable businesspeople everywhere. When we encounter customers such as these, we often find ourselves thinking sympathetically toward mass murderers and chain saw vivisectionists. I contend that this handful of troublemakers (and you know who they are!), are not the bane of commerce that they proport themselves to be. Those customers, the ones who no amount of public relations, no heroic efforts at satisfaction, no going the extra mile will ever satisfy, are not the focus of this book. I am quite prepared to write these people off and to move on to more manageable problems.

The sad truth is that we will always have people who cannot be satisfied, regardless of our efforts. This is not to say that telling a customer to go pound a rock in his ear is ever a reasonable approach to take. Nothing less than 100 percent effort at customer complaint resolution is ever acceptable. In my 25 years of dealing with all segments of the public, I feel justified in saying this. If a sale can be saved, and more importantly, if the customer can be salvaged, and with that salvation, your reputation is left intact, there can be no such thing as too much effort.

Customer/Merchant Relationship

We do not own our customers. That's the plain and short of it. We have them for the time being, and if we're really good at what we do, we may have them for a longer period of time. But we do not own them, and we cannot make them buy from us. How then can we hope to build a business which uses as its base a core of satisfied purchasers? The answer is simply this: **We must treat each customer as he or she wishes to be treated!** Please note, I have not said as **we** wish to be treated, because how we wish to be treated has no bearing on how a customer may wish to be treated.

Consider this: My father is a very formal man. For the 40-odd years he was in business, he addressed most of his customers as Mr. This or Mr. That. He rarely called them by their first names, not because they didn't want him to, but rather because **he** didn't wish to be called by **his** first name! Now this was a fine thing for the people who grew up like my dad, who were reserved and overly polite, but in the day-to-day business world as we find it in the 90s, his insistence on protocol was both counterproductive and old-fashioned. My point is this: my father treated his customers a certain way because he perceived them a certain way. This attitude, while certainly not disrespectful or mean, was in effect self-defeating to his goals, that is, the movement of merchandise. Ignore the golden rule when dealing with customers. Replace it with the platinum rule: **treat each customer as he or she wishes to be treated.**

It is a fact of life, some customers will be happier than others with the same level of service or product. This again harkens back to the concept of each customer is an individual, and the art of customer relations (yes, it is an art), hinges on our recognizing that fact. No two customers are exactly alike, since no two people are exactly alike. We are all composites of that which makes up our world. Our prejudices, our religious background, our political and social beliefs, as well as our educational levels, marriage status, racial background, and economic standing, all roll up into one package. And that package is as individual as our fingerprints. It is ludicrous to insist on treating all customers as if they were all recent extractions from the same cookie sheet.

How then can we know the proper way to react to a particular complaint or problem? Moreover, how can we hope to resolve a customer's dispute without having a preset attitude about the situation? I liken customer complaint resolution to a good paint and body shop. No two accidents are ever identical. The degree of damage to one auto is never exactly the same as the degree of damage to another. But the end result will be. Both vehicles will come into a repair shop dented and smashed. One may have a broken windshield, while the other may have a brake lens cracked. One may have extensive damage to the front end, while the other may have a caved-in door on the passenger side. The point is this: while both cars came in with different complaints, both will leave (ideally) in near-new car condition. The end result is customer satisfaction. While we may arrive there from two totally different directions, the end result is what matters.

What compels a buyer to favor your company over another? It could be an advertisement the customer saw, it could be the location of your store, or perhaps it was just blind luck. But what will keep that customer at your counter is the degree to which he or she is satisfied with the service and product you provide. Few of us sell a product that has no competition. How much nicer it would be if our customers could only buy from us.

But the reality is any product we sell is probably available from a dozen other vendors, and at a dozen different prices. So what about quality? Do we offer our customers a product that never breaks, never develops problems resulting from manufacturers defects, and never falls short of the customer's expectations? Probably not.

In a more perfect world all things would work exactly as we expect them to, and nothing would ever break, wear out, or diminish in value. But this is not a perfect world, and we can fully expect a certain amount of difficulty to result from all products or services we provide.

If defects are inevitable, and if every company has them, then why worry? Because while all products will from time to time cause a problem, the difference between a good company and a great company is the way these problems are resolved.

Perceived Value

Consider what happens when an individual purchases a new car. In most areas all makes of cars are available to the new car buyer. He or she may choose from the least expensive Korean import to the most expensive European model. Between those two extremes lies a virtual plethora of choices. He or she may purchase an automobile in any price range, and within that price range, select any one of dozens of different makes and models. In addition, that same automobile, the exact same model, can be purchased from at least two and often a dozen different dealerships, at as many different prices as there are dealers. How then does any dealer ever succeed in such a competitive arena?

The determining factor in any sale, be it a new car, or a car wash, is perceived value. Whether or not a sale is consummated will depend largely on the prospective customer's perception of how much value she will receive for her money. In the case of the new car, the customer wishes to receive the greatest number of options, and the best selection of color and style, for the minimum outlay of dollars. If a salesperson can convince the customer that an automobile has the most bang for the buck, the deal is as good as done. If not, the customer will look elsewhere for her new car.

Most people would consider $10,000 for a new car to be a reasonable price. Let's look at that $10,000 and what it represents. For $10,000 you could pay for about 7 percent of a nice home in most places in America. For $10,000 you could take a great vacation, around the world, and spend about a month abroad. For $10,000 you could send a child halfway through a college career. So we see $10,000 is a good amount of money. Now, every new car dealer in America also maintains a used car lot. On this lot can be found cars ranging from $500.00 to prices coming close to the new car prices next door. Why would anyone pay $10,000 for a new car when they could save $9,500 buying a used model? The answer? Perceived value!

Perceived value is that value that a new car offers over a used one. A new car provides transportation. A new car is less likely to break down. A new car is less likely to need new tires, new hoses, new belts. A new car tells your friends and associates, "I'm doing quite well, thank you," and reaffirms your confidence in yourself. A used car merely provides transportation. The crux of the matter is this: For $10,000 a buyer may purchase a new car with values he considers to be far and away better than if he'd purchased 20 used cars for $500.00 each!

Customer Killers

The quality of merchandise is a factor in any transaction, either for hard goods or service. Location, hours of operation, methods of payment, and managerial policies all play a part in a customer's decision as to whether to continue patronizing an establishment. But there are two factors that will almost always insure that not only will the customer be sent away unsatisfied, but will in most cases, not return. Both center around the problem of personnel.

The reason personnel play such a pivotal role in customer satisfaction is due largely to the fact customers perceive the person they are dealing with to be vested with full grace and authority to represent the company. This belief, as unreasonable as it may seem, is fostered by the trappings of office. When we are greeted by a car salesperson at an auto dealership, we know (if this isn't our first venture into the world of car buying), that before we're finished, we will also meet the credit manager, the sales manager, probably the used car appraiser, and a host of other people, all of whom will be integral to our purchasing a new car. Yet invariably we will judge the dealership by our assessment of that first individual, the salesperson. If he annoys us, or rubs us the wrong way, chances are we'll end up leaving without really looking in depth at his inventory. Conversely, if he can do that which he is paid to do, namely make us feel at home and predisposed toward him, the dealership has a much better shot at our car dollars.

The second factor concerning personnel is of course the question of continuity. There is a car dealership in Canton, Texas, that boasts of being the largest Chevrolet dealer in Texas without a salesperson. Henry Lewis Chevrolet is literally known throughout the eastern portion of Texas, not because of the lack of salespeople but because the owner is visible and ready to greet all customers. Odds are very good that no matter what time of day you call this dealership Henry Lewis would answer the phone himself. This type of operation is the epitome of continuity of personnel. If the average Chevy buyer were to buy a new car every four years, and were to purchase that car in Canton, Texas, then he or she would deal with the same salesman each time from 1970 up to the present! Customers like this concept because they don't have to go through the process of learning about the seller each time they want to do business with the company.

The side benefit to continuity of personnel is that with longevity comes expertise. The longer a person has been doing a particular job, the more experience that person brings to each transaction. Few of us would like to be the first patient on which a doctor operates, and that truth carries right on down to the fact that few of us want to stand in line while a checker is trained at the market, or have our plumbing worked on by a trainee. The same holds for a new barber or an inexperienced baby sitter. The longer an individual has performed a task, the better we feel about that individual plying his or her trade on our behalf.

There is a spectacular opportunity for business people who realize the importance of employee continuity. The most common complaints employers voice is that good help is hard to find. That's outrageous! In truth, good employees are hard to keep, not hard to find. Employers can't keep good help because good help, like cream, rises to the top. And this is where the opportunity for the business community to score high marks comes in. The longer a business can retain an employee, the better chance it has of maintaining high service standards. There is a direct correlation between high service standards and a high level of customer satisfaction.

The way to raise the degree of commitment to service among your employees is to establish a direct link between customer satisfaction and your employee's compensation package. This can be done is a number of ways, some rather obvious, and expensive, some less obvious, and quite inexpensive.

Rewarding Excellence

As human beings, we thrive on recognition. Even the meanest of clerks sitting in a back room under a dimly lit bulb cranking out projections wants to be patted on the back from time to time. If a company wishes to make service important to the employees, it must first make service important to itself. The concept of "Do as I say, not as I do" will not work in the business world. Let employees see the company's commitment to excellence, not just as a slogan but as a way of life, and they will follow. But let it be perceived as just another piece of fluff, a ball of hype, and all the posters and slogans in the world won't get it off the ground.

The place to start a campaign for service excellence is at the top. The president or the general manager of a business must first make the announcement that service is now the primary function of the business. And this announcement should not be made casually, or even within the framework of regular company meetings. There is a sound reason for this. In many companies, a commitment to excellent service is a given. In others, it is an assumption. Management assumes that their employees know the importance of friendliness, courtesy, and prompt service. And it is these companies, these that seem to assume all clerks are created friendly, that often find themselves with the highest incident of customers in crisis.

By holding a special meeting to announce the change in policy and focus, and by placing emphasis on this attitudinal shift in objective, management is underlying the memo with large, bold print! They are saying in essence, **"THIS IS IMPORTANT. PAY ATTENTION!"** It is important, and to treat it like any other policy change, such as what identification is required for check cashing, or how many days pass before an exchange of merchandise is prohibited, is ludicrous.

There is in Texas a grocery chain that teaches all employees, from baggers to store managers, that each customer is to be greeted and given a friendly smile. I have been in many of their stores, and the same greeting was given in each store by every employee I met. My first reaction was one of incredulous disbelief. No company can have that many friendly employees. After a few visits, my perspective changed to observation. I wondered if they ever got tired of saying, "Hi. Welcome to our store." The tactic, however, took its toll on me. Soon, whenever I visited one of their competitors, the first thing I noticed was how unfriendly they seemed to be. Mind you, they were not overtly hostile. Quite the contrary. They were very matter-of-fact in their dealings with me. I came, I bought, and I left. But I longed for the smile, the friendly face of their competitors. Where do you think I shop now?

How can a manager instill that type of service oriented mindset in employees? First, by example. Paste a smile on your face until it becomes second nature. Speak to employees who seem to be less than enthusiastic about their job. Maybe they're in the wrong one. Point that out to them. Second, hold contests. Make a friendly competition out of being friendly. In the case of a product oriented company, such as grocery stores, clothing outlets, even discount merchandisers, stores that maintain large staffs, staffs comprised of employees of varying degrees of importance ranging from stockers to department managers, to general managers, put into effect some sort of system for recognizing the friendliest employee of the week or month. Place his or her picture in the break area, or better yet, in the front of the store, identifying the employee by name and department, with a brief explanation of why he or she is being cited. This does not have to be expensive or elaborate. But it does have to be noticeable and consistent. To pack the recognition with some real punch, add a small monetary reward, either in the form of a bonus check, or perhaps a gift certificate for use in the store. The more tangible the reward is, the more real the efforts will be. If your firm employs 50 people, and your company awards the employee of the month a cash stipend of $100 each month, you will in effect be paying each employee fifty cents a week to smile at customers, and by extension, you will be giving your customers a novelty they may not have seen in decades: A willing worker!

The happy employee with a shining face and outgoing smile will give your customers something else: confidence in your company's commitment to making them happy, too. The customer will pick up quickly on the attitude of the employee, and that attitude will play positively when the customer is considering a purchase, or when, in the future, he or she is considering where to go to spend money. And all this for fifty cents a week.

There is one other fringe benefit to this approach. Most people who hold a job do so with mixed feelings. On the one hand, they are glad they can work, glad they have the opportunity to earn a living. On the other hand, they cannot help but feel a certain degree of neglect on the part of their employer. I have never been disappointed later in any of my employees who I cited for their positive attitude. How many times have we all heard the expression "one big, happy family?" It's just words until it comes home in the form of special recognition. While this concept works in any type of business, it works especially well in service related areas, places like retail stores, restaurants and business which provide one on one type customer service. It encourages the strong to work harder, and gives hope to the weak that they might improve their performance.

In Parting . . .

Satisfied customers are the essence of any successful on-going enterprise. But before a company can hope to build a rapport between itself and its customers, attention must be given to the underlying philosophy of service and to what extent the company is prepared to go to assure that the service their employees provide is at the highest possible degree. Trust, mutual respect, and a basic sense of integrity running through a company will find manifestation in the customer's awareness of the importance the company has made to providing service on a grand scale.

2

The Importance of Procedure

Obviously, not all complaints are of the same level of urgency. A customer might wish to point out a light bulb designed to last 1,000 hours only made it through the weekend. Another might want to report that the television they purchased last month suddenly caught fire, and destroyed not only the owner's dwelling but an additional 341 other apartments in the process. One of these problems can be handled by a manager. The other will require the attention of the chairman of the board!

If a procedure is in place before the customer complains, then that complaint will be dispatched quickly and efficiently, much like the aforementioned school fire drill. One of the tenets of good customer relations is that all problems be addressed quickly. This is not to say the resolution of that problem will be quick; many times that just isn't possible. But often the mere appearance of action or concern will temporarily hold a customer's anger at bay. Do not misunderstand this statement.

There is no point in trying to pull wool over a customer's eyes. If it is your store's policy to take no action in a particular situation, tell your customer this immediately. There is no such thing as waiting out a customer relation problem. A customer in crisis is more like a dead fish than a bottle of wine. Fish do not improve with age, they only become more intense.

Spreading the Pain

We're going to visit our three "special" businesses and set up problems not unlike those faced everyday by businesses around the world. As you read these scenarios, you will find yourself "pre-solving" the issues. The only wrong answers here are the ones that result in the customer leaving your store, never to return.

Scenario # 1

Ernest Ernie's Electronics sells batteries. All shapes and sizes, all voltages and prices. One particular battery sells for $3.49 for a package of four. Janet, a sales person at Ernest Ernie's sold a package of these batteries to a customer. He paid cash for them and left the store, headed for home. The next day, the customer returned to the store, batteries in hand, and told a different clerk, (Janet wasn't in the store) that he'd purchased these batteries the day before, and they would not work. The clerk tested the batteries, and as the customer claimed, they were dead.

How do we resolve this situation? To begin with, there is no way of ascertaining that the batteries the customer has in his hand are indeed the batteries he bought last night. Since most batteries show no external signs of wear, for all practical purposes, these may well have been the older set, the set that the new ones replaced. Second, the nature of batteries is such that the customer may have accidently drained them himself, and now wishes to feign ignorance and pass the responsibility to the store. In either case, the clerk is now standing in front of a customer who claims he was sold defective merchandise, and now wants the situation resolved.

Scenario # 2

Dead-Kill Bugstore operates a national chain of locally owned franchises. Their claim to fame is that they sell a contract for $79.95 plus a $19.95 monthly service charge. For this amount, Dead-Kill sprays a home, inside and out, and maintains monthly visits designed to keep bugs from coming back. They guarantee that you won't see a bug, or they'll come out immediately and respray, regardless of the time of month, and without regard to the next regularly scheduled service call.

Bill is the closer for the company. He's just sold a contract to an elderly woman to protect her home from roaches and other bugs. The morning after the first application, and the application that will be the most through by virtue of the nature of the exterminating business, Bill answers the phone to find an extremely upset woman screaming about her dead cat. She tells Bill that she's canceling the contract, and moreover, contacting her lawyer about bring a lawsuit for the wrongful death of her animal, not to mention the mental and physical strain this whole incident has placed on her.

The customer is certain the cat is dead because of excessive use of chemicals. Moreover, the welfare of the cat was a specific concern of the customer, and she had asked Bill if the chemicals they were planning to use were toxic to animals. She had plainly stated her fears for her animal's life, and now, despite Bill's assurances to the contrary, she had lost one of her prize pets. It is evident to her that not only did Bill not care about her, and not care about her animals, but that his only real concern was taking her money.

Scenario # 3

Sell-More is an up-and-coming chain of retail department stores, regional in scope, and usually located in malls. They are growth conscious, and have maintained that the ideal employees are homegrown, coming up through the ranks, and finally getting to prove themselves by managing their own stores. Though they are a large chain, they have maintained the small town touch by using quaint, old-fashioned terminology such as "the jeans patch," for their blue jean department, and "cookin' stuff" for their kitchenwares department, and insisting that all employees wear name tags with their first name only.

Sell-More prides itself on carrying national brands. In their shoe department they sell a name brand sneaker that can be bought in three different stores in the mall. But because of their marketing positions and strategies, they retail this shoe for $44.95, while other stores are selling the same shoe for $39.95. This fact has made their store a target for people who buy shoes in one outlet for $39.95, then return them to Sell-More for a $44.95 refund.

Rita is the department manager of the shoe area and has under her supervision a staff of 10 workers. No more than three are ever on the floor at one time, and most of the time that number is two. Rita looks up to find a man standing in front of her, holding a paper sack. He extracts from the sack a wet pair of tennis shoes of the aforementioned brand. He points out that his wife washed the shoes, which he says were purchased two months ago, and that when she did, the green leather trim bled over to the canvas uppers. He does not have his receipt. Rita is concerned because she has no proof that the man truly bought the shoes in her store. Second, she cannot ascertain how old the shoes are. Third, for all she knows, the man may have stolen the shoes just moments ago, taken them to the rest room, poured water on them, and is now trying to scam her for a total refund.

All three of these scenarios deal with different problems, but all three have at their root the same common denominator: dissatisfied customers. The proper resolution of all three situations will vary from store to store, from locale to locale. But there is a common thread which could have made these three situations easier to resolve. And that thread is the establishment of a procedure in advance of the need. The interesting thing is that it matters not what the problem is, all that matters is that the procedure be in place. Once guidelines are set, and procedures are ready, all customer complaints will be handled in a like manner. An organized plan, in place before it is needed, will allow your company the luxury of acting on complaints, instead of reacting to problems. There are four basic steps in preparing a procedure schedule for problems.

Establish Channels of Authority

First, and certainly the most obvious step toward the successful resolution of the crisis customer, is to establish channels of authority. These channels will not necessarily be the same as the actual chain of command already in place within an organization. In larger operations it most likely will not be. The purpose of this channel of authority is to help establish the procedure for taking a crisis customer out of the mainstream of events and channelling him or her into the area where immediate resolution may be rendered. Moreover, with a chain of command in place, and with people authorized to perform the delicate task of customer problem resolution, the natural hesitancy many employees exhibit in regard to "sticking their neck out" disappears. The resolution of problems is their job, and they will approach it with the same confidence they display when handling any other facet of their employment.

Depending on the size of your organization, from one to three people should be at the top of the team heading up your problem customer group. I have seen this team called by many names, and strongly suggest that your company affix a special designation to these workers. Choose a name that fits your corporate image. Some names that might serve well are:

- The Fix-It Squad
- Fix-It-Right-Team
- Customer Advocates
- Customer Satisfaction Team
- Get-it-Right-Team

You may want to customize these, or find designations that will speak to the purpose of your organization. But make no mistake about one thing. These people are an elite group. Your company must entrust them with the power to correct a situation, without a great deal of delay, and without the fear of constantly being second guessed by management. This concept leaves some managers quaking in their corporate boots. The idea of vesting other employees with the authority to correct mistakes without higher supervision is enough to send the traditional "tight reigned" manager into spasms! Training, therefore, becomes the order of the day. Employees, properly trained, will tend to find the correct solutions to the vast majority of problems. If they should make a mistake, if they should issue a refund when none was due, or exchange merchandise that was not eligible for exchange, your store must balance those *faux pas* against the greater savings of customer satisfaction and efficient time management.

It is an unfortunate truth that customers are unpredictable when it comes to wanting mistakes made right. If this were a more perfect world, the customer would only require the time and expertise of your resolution manager during the times when he or she is on duty. But more than one person needs to be trained for this post, and the training must insure standardized treatment of all customer complaints.

Let's look at our three scenarios. In each case the problem was brought to the attention either of the clerk on duty, or the salesperson who sold the contract. These people were placed in the position of either rectifying a mistake made by someone else, or venturing out to unknown territory to correct a situation. How wrong that is! In every case, and particularly in the case of the irate customer whose batteries had proved defective, a properly trained customer relations specialist could have made the difference between an unhappy customer and a satisfied buyer.

Developing the Proper Paperwork

Paperwork is the bane of commerce! But unless you operate a one-person organization, paper trails are often the only means a resolution manager will have for following a problem from a historic prospective. The need for accurate records stem from three different areas, the historic prospective of the product, the history of the customer, and the need to be able to plan future purchases of the same product.

Historic Perspective of the Product

Some items are more problematic than others. This is true in most industries, regardless of their orientation. In the electronics industry, wire typically is problem free, while car stereo amplifiers are the proverbial products from hell. The more complex the product, and the newer the concept, the more "bugs" it is likely to have. When compact disks were first introduced in car stereos, one in three malfunctioned. Compare that figure to a similar radio but one containing a conventional cassette deck, and the failure rate drops to one in 29. Now compare those figures to ordinary car stereos, without any auxiliary decks, equipped with only standard FM and AM tuners, and the defect rates drops to one in 350!

It is obvious that some products will be the subject of complaints more often than others. With proper paper work, and an organized approach to classifying complaints, the historic prospective becomes clearer. Let's consider the three sample companies and see how they each could have made use of a complaint file from the prospective of the product's history.

When faced with a customer who claimed the batteries purchased last night were dead when he got home with them, the clerk had two options. He could have risked being the victim of a scam and losing money for the company, or he could risk losing the customer for all time. If Ernest Ernie's Electronics had already designated a customer resolution manager, then the first thing the clerk would have done was turn the problem over to the designated employee.

The resolution manager's first action would have been to listen thoroughly to the customer's complaint. Her next action would have been to check the history file on this particular product. If in checking the file, she were to see that in the last three weeks, three other customers had complained of similar problems with this particular brand of battery, than the next step is obvious: replace the batteries for the customer, or refund his money, whichever he is requesting, and note the problem in the complaint ledger.

Two things are accomplished here. First, the customer's complaint is treated with more attention than it might otherwise have gotten. The minute the resolution manager realized she was dealing with a recurring problem, it took the problem out of the realm of speculation and placed it firmly in the area of reality. This customer was in all likelihood not pulling a fast one on Ernest Ernie's. He was not only in the right, but in reality, he was the victim of someone's inattention to detail. And his consternation and righteous anger is justified.

Second, and perhaps of greater importance, the resolution manager now is aware that a problem is occurring in the battery department. A certain percentage of batteries is leaving the store defective. As bad as it may be to have an irate customer in your place of business complaining about the quality of your merchandise or services, it is far worse when that same customer doesn't come back to offer the store a chance to make amends. Who would you rather deal with, a customer on the premises who is unhappy with an aspect of your service, or a customer going about town telling all his friends, relatives, employees and associates that your place is a front for organized crime money laundering, and that the goods and services your company provides are shoddy and second rate?

Armed with the statistics of an increasing number of customer complaints dealing with a particular product, your store can take the necessary steps to rectify the problem. Without the benefit of a historical journal, the true defective rate of an individual product might never come to light.

The historical journal should consist of loose leaf pages, and the page should look like this:

PRODUCT COMPLAINT SURVEY
PRODUCT INFORMATION

Date : May 12, 1993

Product:

Generic:	Batteries
Brand:	Duracell
Model:	Alkaline
Size:	AAA
Lot #:	C-1009

Manufacturer:	Mallory
Vendor:	First State Wholesale

CUSTOMER INFORMATION

Customer:	George Wilson
Address:	1414 Canyon Road
City:	Chicago
Phone:	(312) 555-8106
Nature of Complaint:	Batteries dead when purchased
Customer requested :	Replacement of batteries
Complaint Resolution:	Gave customer new batteries

Historic Charting of a Specific Customer's Complaint Activity

This sheet should be completely filled out at the time of the customer complaint. Customers often resent having to give specifics concerning themselves beyond their name, and in some cases, don't even wish to give that. And in all fairness, this is not unreasonable from the standpoint that such information is not germane to the problem at hand. Your resolution manager, however, should be able to elicit most of the needed information by gently implying that action to correct the problem cannot commence until the store has a total handle on the problem, and this information is necessary to render the service or resolution the customer requests.

The second part of this form, Customer Information, is needed to establish if a customer is a habitual complainer, or refund seeker, and to also help with the follow-up letter you will send after the problem is resolved. (More about the follow-up letter later in this chapter.)

Accurate Verification and Identification of Defective Products and Services

As we will discuss later in this book, these journals will be instrumental in developing buying strategies. They will replace the casual statements often heard in department meetings that begin, "gosh, we seem to have a lot of defective batteries all of a sudden" or "and I think we need to look into the freshness of our battery supply. A lot of the salespeople are complaining about irate customers."

With accurate complaint journals, not only will your service department have a more realistic handle on the problems attendant to certain goods or services, but the entire organization, from purchasing to sales, will have a firmer grasp on where problems lie, and what can be done to mitigate or eliminate them. Nothing beats hard facts, and nothing generates them better than hard copies of complaint journals.

An extra bonus these journals will provide is the actual statistics of product failure that will be available to those employees who deal directly with the vendors or sales representatives who call on your company. They can often be used when negotiating a price or a return policy. In the case of the battery problem, for example, many vendors are hesitant to accept any returns on batteries for the same reasons the clerk was initially hesitant to make the refund. Armed with the complaint journal, however, it would take a particularly stubborn rep to ignore the realities of this problem, especially if all the batteries in question were to have originated from the same lot number or specific model type.

Now let's look at the journal page concerning the poor cat who met his Maker prematurely.

CUSTOMER COMPLAINT SURVEY
INFORMATION

Date : May 12, 1992

CUSTOMER INFORMATION

Customer:	Emma Lou Powell
Address:	2828 South Valley Drive
City:	Denver
Phone:	(303) 555-3433

Nature of Complaint:	Cat died after we sprayed premises.
Customer requested:	Customer screaming on phone, incoherently.
Complaint Resolution:	Explained to customer that there is nothing in our pesticide that would hurt her pets. Also advised company attorney of situation.

Additional actions:	Offered to replace the cat with either a new kitten or an older cat, and told Mrs. Powell I understood how bad she must feel, as I too have lost pets. It seemed to comfort her a bit.
Service Performed:	We sprayed her house for roaches and ants.
Chemical Used:	Dursband
Quantity Used:	Three pounds over a 2,000 square foot area
Method of Application:	Spray and dusting
Manufacturer:	Acme Chemical
Vendor:	Triple G Chemicals

This customer complaint survey will have an additional impact that the first example did not. It will serve as a memo to the file in the event the customer does make good on her threat to sue the company. By no means definitive, the report's existence serves to point out that complaints of this or any other nature are taken seriously by the company, and that an effort was made to satisfy the complainant. It would also be helpful if no other unexplained cat deaths were on hand in the event the entire complaint journal is subpoenaed for examination by the court. The lack of other such complaints will help prove your contention that the actions of the company could not have caused the death of the house cat, inasmuch as other clients have also had house cats and they have never complained about those cats dying when your company treated the homes they lived in. While this is not sufficient evidence of innocence, it certainly is a post upon which your lawyers will be able to hang a reasonable amount of doubt, which may well be the deciding factor in any court action.

Establishing a Customer Resolution Area

One of the tenets of quick resolution involves the precept that a complaining customer is one who has the chance of drawing too much attention to him or herself. To that end, it is prudent to have an area of the store set up to handle those customers whose complaints may reach the ears of other customers. This segregation of the crisis customer should not be obvious, but rather done for the purpose of resolving his or her complaint quickly and smoothly.

Besides removing the crisis customer from within earshot of other customers, a problem resolution area will also serve as the area in which your customer resolution team can work with some degree of organization toward resolving the customer's complaint.

This area should be relatively clutter free, certainly not in the same region of the store that defective products are stored (nothing like adding fuel to the fire), and it is probably best if a table with a few chairs can be provided. The term for this area should be one of endearment, something along the line of the hospitality room, or the customer reception area. Avoid referring to it as the problem room, or any other negative designation, even when just speaking about it among employees.

Negative concepts are carried from negative images, and to refer to this area in anything less than a positive manner will doom your project before it starts.

A word of caution. Whatever site you select to perform triage on your customer's problems, it should not be too obscure a location. Many customers may be nervous about going down a long hallway, into a dimly lit room at the end of the hall. This sense of uneasiness will be magnified if the customer relations specialist and the customer in question happen to be of the opposite gender. The area selected to serve as your resolution area need not be a separate room, or even in a separate part of the store. It need only be away from the main flow of traffic.

In the event the space is available, and the other previously stated criteria are present, an area designated the problem resolution room should contain, among other amenities, a coffee and soft drink machine, comfortable chairs, perhaps even a few plants, and space permitting, a fish tank. Yes, that's right, a fish tank. There are few things more soothing to the agitated psyche than the sight of fish swimming contentedly in a protected environment. Also, it is an excellent idea if music of a soft and gentle nature is piped into the area.

Once your customer is safely away from the mainstream of your other business activity, begin the interview by stating the position of the store: that is, express how interested the management of the store is in seeing that all customers are treated well, and that the satisfaction of the customer is the primary reason why the store is in business. It would not do any harm, and it may well go a long way to support what you have said if you identify yourself as the store's customer relations person, or in any other manner that would indicate to the customer that your company is so serious about attaining 100 percent satisfaction for its customers that a special procedure has been established for dealing with problems that arise from time to time. But avoid giving the impression that you handle so many complaints each day that a separate unit was needed just to catalog them all.

In Parting . . .

Just as no one would attempt to build a home or construct a model airplane without first looking at the plans and making sure all parts and pieces were present before work began, companies cannot hope to put into effect any sort of customer relations department without first establishing a blueprint, or a plan of action. To insure a successful customer problem resolution department, be certain each employee knows what part he or she is to play, including being familiar with the paperwork, and the procedure involved in customer problem resolution.

3

Determine the Minimum Requirement To Solve the Crisis

Not all dissatisfied customers expect heroic efforts to correct their problem. And to always take such steps is not only foolish, but downright cost prohibitive. There are many times when all a customer wishes to do is express disappointment in the service or product they have received, and be assured that it won't happen again. Remember the light bulb problem in Chapter 2. Light bulbs are supposed to last 1,000 hours. This isn't a terribly long time if they are left on day and night, but certainly a bulb should go three months or so with normal use.

If a customer were to complain that the bulbs he bought in your store two months ago seemed to burn out more quickly than he'd expected, there would be no need to replace the bulbs for him. He may merely have been making conversation. If, however, he appeared in your store, a sack of burned out bulbs in his hand, and wanted to speak to the manager, this is an entirely different case. In such a situation the customer clearly expects some sort of action on the part of the store to correct what he perceives as a defective merchandise problem. The semantics of problem resolution are as important as any other aspect. Let's listen as the store manager talks with the unhappy light bulb buyer.

Scenario # 4

"I'd like to speak to the manager, please."

"I'm the manager."

"I'm not happy with these light bulbs."

"What seems to be the problem?"

"They didn't last the time it said they would on the box they came in."

"I see. Do you have your receipt?"

So far, in less than 10 seconds, the manager of the store has done three things wrong. And he's only spoken three times! Point one, when he identified himself as the manager, he did not identify himself personally. What difference did that make? For starters, he has already signalled to the customer that this is a matter between the customer and the store, and the store is bigger than the customer. The store doesn't need an introduction; by virtue of it's sheer size, it wins! How much better the initial meeting would have been if the store manager had extended his hand in greeting and introduced himself not only as the store manager, but also as a human being.

Second, he placed the customer on notice by asking what "seems" to be the problem. This is the same as a doctor asking the patient, "What's your problem now?" See the tone? A much more diplomatic approach to the situation would have been to ask the customer, "How may I help you?" or even, "May I be of assistance?" Either response is preferable to the unspoken accusation that the problem is an imaginary one, existing only in the mind of the customer.

We know that body language is an important aspect of our daily lives. Picture a man with his arms folded across his chest, his back stiffened, his eyes narrowed, and his brow furrowed, with one eye brow raised, and then picture yourself telling that person that you have a problem that requires his help in resolution. Probably not! Now picture the same man, but he is smiling, his hands are open, and his arms are at his side. Can you approach him? Most certainly. And when you do, you do so with a much less guarded manner. You are not openly hostile, because he is not hostile. There is room, you imagine, to negotiate your problem.

The third mistake our manager made was in asking for a receipt. This in itself is an appropriate question. The only thing wrong here was the timing. In asking if the customer had his receipt, he was throwing down the gauntlet, setting the parameters for the confrontation. He was in essence saying, "Okay, Bub, let's see what you've got! Show me your legal standing before I invest any more time with your worthless case!"

What a bad image. Remember, you've spent hundreds of dollars to get this guy into your store, and now, in less than 10 seconds, you've revealed your true nature, and more damaging than that, you've revealed the true nature of your company. You have been reserved, suspicious, and hostile. From the customer's standpoint, he's on his own from this point on, and it's every man for himself! Let's go back.

Scenario # 4 (started over)

"I'd like to speak to the manager, please."

"I'm the manager. Ralph Jennings. (Hand extended, smile on face) How can I help you?"

If you have extended your hand, and he has taken it, when you tell the customer your name, he will in most cases tell you his. You are no longer dealing with a stranger, and most importantly, neither is your customer.

"Mr. Jennings, my name is Rick Blaine, and I'm not happy with these light bulbs."

"Oh, what's wrong with them?"

"They didn't last the time it said they would on the box they came in."

"I see. When did you buy them?"

See the difference? Your customer is disarmed. He was expecting a confrontation, a hostile encounter, but you offered to shake hands, offered your name, and every question you asked was pointed toward the direction of solving his problem, not assessing blame or guilt.

Scenario # 4 (continued)

"I bought these last month, around the third. The box said they'd last 1,000 hours. Now I've only had them five weeks, and four of the six I bought are already burned out. I think they should have lasted longer than that."

"It would seem so, wouldn't it, Mr. Blaine. Do you happen to have your receipt?"

"I threw it out. I've never had a problem with light bulbs before."

"And you're sure you bought these only five weeks ago?"

"Yeah, I bought them the same time I had my car tuned in your shop. I probably still have the receipt for the tune-up. I save those for tax purposes."

"Oh, that's alright. Let's see, you've had the bulbs for five weeks, and even if you used them day and night, that would only come to around 800 hours. What would you like me to do to make this right for you?"

"Well, could you replace them?"

"I can. Let me get you some new ones."

Clearly, the customer had received some value from the burned out bulbs. And just as clearly, the store was entitled to some percentage of the sale for value received. But we are talking about light bulbs, items that sell 4/1.99! If Jennings had wanted to be picky, he could have calculated the time the bulbs were in use, (a point the customer would have disagreed with) calculated what percentage of that time would be covered by the warranty, (840 hours of possible use, discounting 50 percent of the time for daylight, leaving 420 hours of use, hence making the bulbs only 58 percent defective, and working out the value of 58 percent of 1.99 equals .84 worth of value received, adjusting the new bulbs to a value of $1.15).

To calculate such a discount on the new bulbs would have been economically correct, but in the realm of customer relations, it would have been a disaster! The time it would take to explain the mathematics to the customer, haggle over the precise amount of actual bulb usage time involved, and figure to the penny what the prorated value of the time left unburned in each bulb would have been to expose the manager and the store to the meanest of criticism. If the aim was to make the customer regard the store in the smallest of terms, Jennings would have accomplished that goal. If the goal was to allow himself and his your store to appear gracious, to appear concerned with the customer's satisfaction, than he'd have fallen far short of that mark.

Moreover, consider the actual value of a manager's time. If he is compensated at the rate of $30,000.00 per year, that makes each working day worth $115.38, each working minute worth twenty-four cents. If a manager were to spend five minutes on this problem, he's already cost his company $1.20 in salary. $1.20 to solve a $1.15 problem. The point is that there is such a thing as being penny wise and dollar foolish! In addition to costing the store the potential of a customer in the future, the actual cost in salary to the manager exceeded the liability of this transaction! What a loser this could have been. But by asking the customer what action he'd like taken, and by determining that the problem could be resolved by replacing four light bulbs with new ones, Manager Jennings is a hero.

Customer Blaine, when he returns to work on Monday, will probably tell all his co-workers, all his customers, and all the people he deals with that day about the service he received at the Big-Buck Discount store last Saturday night. Instead of telling people what a rip-off Bright-light bulbs are, he'll spend his time telling people how courteously he was treated "by the MANAGER, no less!" As a problem resolver, Jennings can take pride in such successes and the fact that because of his efforts, customer Blaine will be back again.

Performing Triage in the Complaint Department

There are some who say being an astronaut is a tough job. Others say lion taming is the most dangerous occupation of modern times. Balderdash! The most dangerous job in America today is held by the poor clerk who mans the customer service desk of a discount store the first business morning after Christmas Day! Triage is the act of knowing when a customer is in crisis, and when he or she is merely looking for a quick solution to a temporary problem. For example, here are three customers, all three of whom are in the store at the same time, all three of whom have problems. The first has a flashlight with a cracked lens. The second has a color television that will only pick up radio signals. The third has the charred remains of a toaster/oven he claims is responsible for the burning deaths of 16 people living in the apartment above him when it malfunctioned, causing his apartment building to burn to the ground. Who is in crisis here?

Oddly enough, it is the customer with the flashlight. The problem with the television is outside the scope of the customer resolution manager. It will be consigned to the service department, where it will either be repaired or replaced. All that is necessary here is to fill out the forms, and call for someone to pick up the unit. The poor devil with the toaster is a case for the company attorney, not for civilians. In fact, one of the cardinal rules of customer complaint resolution is never admit fault or blame. It is alright to agree with the customer that his problem is serious, it is fine to help find an amenable solution, but it is clearly outside the parameters of the resolution manager to accept the blame or responsibility for the company.

The guy with the flashlight is the problem customer. Why? Because his problem is one of minor annoyance, more than major expense, and as such, there is a much higher risk of his problem being ignored. (Not now, man, can't you see this guy's got a killer toaster?) Clearly, the man with the flashlight is in present danger of being taken too lightly. He will probably be handed a new flashlight, and sent on his way.

Good? No. Bad. Very bad. Let's reconstruct the scene here. The customer received a flashlight as a gift. It had a broken lens. The customer must now travel to your store which may be out of his way, and certainly was not on his plans for the day prior to opening his gift and stand in a line, waiting to receive what he should have received in the first place, a working flashlight. Do you think his heart grows kinder toward your business as he stands in that line, waiting, waiting, waiting? Probably not. The whole episode is turning into a fiasco. The longer he waits, the less kindly disposed he is toward your store. How can this be avoided? Going on the assumption that your store did not know the lens was cracked, or that the particular model the customer is returning is not listed in your complaint journal as a habitual violator, there was little you could have done to avoid the problem. The only option open now is to make the return process as expedient and painless as possible.

One of the more tangible skills managers of large grocery chains possess is the ability to facilitate and expedite the movement of customers through the check out lane. Consider this option when faced with long lines of customers waiting for any type of service, whether it be to pay for purchases, or exchange defective or unwanted merchandise: position your employees where they can be most effective. Be sure you have at least one customer problem resolution manager on duty at all times, and drill into the minds of your employees, time and time again, the utter importance of fast, friendly service.

Analyze Minimum Action Required to Resolve the Crisis

Once the triage has been completed, determine the minimum and maximum ranges of options at your disposal to resolve the customer's complaint. Bear in mind, not every customer complaint will be resolved to his or her satisfaction. If your enter into the negotiations with an open mind, but one in which parameters of resolution are already firmly in place, you will find arriving at a resolution is a much simpler manner. Let's revisit the Sell-More department store.

When we established their scenario, we used the example of the leather and canvas tennis shoes that had bled dye from the leather to the canvass the first time they were washed. Our customer is taking the position that the shoes should not have bled and wants the store to do something about the situation. The saleswoman who is handling the crisis customer is concerned over the lack of a sales slip, knowing that particular brand is available in many stores, and in at least two others in her own mall. Without a receipt, she is not certain the shoes came from her store to begin with.

The folly here is that it doesn't matter where the shoes came from, the only problem is what the customer wants the store to do. Let's listen.

Scenario # 5

"Do you have a receipt, sir?"

"No. We paid cash for the shoes, about two months ago, and didn't keep the register ticket. But I don't want a refund, all I want is for my daughter to be able to use her shoes."

"Well, sir, without a receipt, I have no way of knowing that you really bought them here. I'm sure you understand."

"All I understand is that I paid forty dollars for a pair of shoes my daughter can't wear. Now what are you going to do about it?"

What indeed? Where did this encounter begin to go wrong? The first question the saleswoman asked was if there was documentation for the sale itself. A natural question, and one which would have made the resolution considerably less confrontational if a receipt had been available. But the lack of paper documentation would not in and of itself cause the crisis customer to walk away empty handed. At least not insofar as he's concerned. He explained he'd paid cash for the product. Moreover, he's also already indicated his willingness to forego a refund in favor of the company replacing the defective shoes. But the saleswoman isn't listening. She is still stuck on the first question.

As if all this wasn't bad enough, as if the customer isn't already annoyed that for forty dollars what he really got was a cheap pair of shoes, now he's being subjected to the saleswoman actually doubting his veracity. She has as good as called him a liar, lumping him in with every ne'er-do-well in the county, and then had the audacity to excuse her suspicions by adding, "I'm sure you understand." No, he does not understand, nor does he appreciate her particular problems with people ripping off the store. His only concern, and one upon which he is very focused at this point, is the defective pair of size seven tennis shoes for which he paid forty dollars.

There is one more subtle but certainly equally offensive factor at work here. Look again at what the saleswoman said to the customer. "I have no way of knowing." She has taken what was business problem and made it personal. Very personal! What she is saying could be expressed in another manner.

What could be done here to facilitate this problem? There are four factors to consider. The nature of the problem, the nature of the product, the nature of the customer, and the nature of the store.

The Nature of the Problem

The problem, as stated by the customer, is that the shoes have bled green dye onto the white canvass. This contention is easily verified. The evidence of the event is in the saleswoman's hands. She is looking at a pair of tennis shoes which have green dye seeping from what is obviously green leather. The complaint and the problem are indeed legitimate.

The Nature of the Product

Further visual examination will provide evidence that the shoes are about two months old. This conclusion is based on the wear, or lack thereof, found on the sole of the shoe. They are obviously not brand new, as some wear is evident. This fact should help substantiate what the customer is claiming, and help refute the thoughts in the saleswoman's mind that the customer had stolen the shoes from the display, taken them into the bathroom, soaked them in the sink, and is now trying to con the store into a refund.

Hand-in-hand with the visual evidence to be considered, is the fact that these particular shoes are backed by a one-year guarantee. Now that warranty is not contingent on the shoes having been sold from this particular outlet, or even from a particular chain. The manufacturer stands ready to make the shoes good, whether they are sent in by the Sell-More department store or the Fast Buck discount outlet. So the reality of the thing is that Sell-More is not on the hook for the shoes in the first place. They have recourse through the manufacturer. The shoes are clearly defective, and as such, clearly eligible for warranty.

The Nature of the Customer

The customer did not ask for a refund. What he did ask for, a request the saleswoman ignored, was that his daughter be able to wear undamaged shoes. He wanted the shoes replaced. The fact that he did not request a refund seems to negate the idea that he was merely trying to pick up a profit by returning the shoes to a higher priced store. There are customers who make their livelihood harassing stores, finding nit-picky things wrong, and then attempting to embarrass or intimidate management into taking a course of action that enriches the customer, while impoverishing the vendor. Clearly, this customer was not one of those.

The Nature of the Store

Businesses are like people. Their reputation proceeds them wherever they go. It is because of that reputation that you are interested enough in customer service to read this and other books on the subject of problem resolution. Consider again the case of Sell-More department store. They obviously maintain a high quality inventory, sell at prices which could be considered higher than the norm, and just as obviously, are enjoying a period of growth and expansion. It is absolute folly to allow any one employee to stand in the way of that forward growth! While it is incumbent upon the workers to realize what the company's goals and long term plans are, and to work within the framework of those plans, it is equally incumbent upon management to instill within their work force an appreciation and understanding of those plans.

Seldom will a business prosper without giving careful consideration to its reputation and long-range image. Entire industries have sprung up to aid and assist the image refinement of the businesses of the '90s. Public relations firms, advertising agencies, even corporate image consultants have grown and prospered solely within the climate of customer services.

If your company will make its goals the goals of its workers, there will be little room for the type of salesperson who will stand in front of a customer, call the customer a liar, and admonish him to "understand" the position of the company.

Determining a Proper Course of Action

Just as not all customers are the same, not all solutions to customers' complaints will be the same either. The solution for any activity will depend on the answer to three questions. First, does a problem really exist? Second, can the customer be satisfied? Third, will the company be willing to do what is necessary to resolve the problem?

Does a Problem Really Exist?

This is not as simple a question as you might imagine. Obviously, a situation exists, or the customer would not now be standing before you with the defective merchandise, the unfulfilled contract, or the dead cat. But the mere fact that a situation has presented itself does not in and of itself constitute a legitimate complaint.

A customer confronts a grocery store manager, and in his or her hand is a piece of summer salami, which the customer claims is spoiled. The manager examines the meat, and notices the expiration tag is dated two months ago. Clearly the meat is spoiled, but that does not mean the customer has a legitimate complaint. Had the product been consumed in a timely way, there is no doubt that the problem would never have existed. The customer, however, either is unaware of or unwilling to acknowledge the origin of the problem, that is, the product has outlived its shelf life.

The manager is faced with this problem. Does he replace a $6.49 sausage, and take the full loss, or does he refuse to handle the situation, thereby facing the possibility of losing the customer for life? On one hand, the store is clearly not responsible for this problem. The meat was sold before the expiration date, but the customer failed to consume it on time. The customer, however, is insisting that inasmuch as the sausage was packed in an air tight wrapper, and had just been opened, the product should have lasted considerably longer. What should be management's actions?

In surveying 26 grocery stores, ranging from small stores to supermarkets, the answer to the question was always the same. Replace or refund. Period. Never once did a store manager indicate that there could be any other course of action. And the reasoning was always the same. Why risk losing a weekly or twice weekly customer over one piece of meat? The down side (that of losing a customer forever) was too great, the upside (saving a $6.49 refund) was not worth the risk. Moreover, the fact that the customer returned the product indicated that in the customer's eyes this was indeed a defective item.

In Parting . . .

Often, people just want to help. It is in this vein that many people complain to stores and businesses about what they perceive to be shortcomings of those enterprises. It is important to listen to what the customer is saying, but it is equally important to listen to how they're saying it. Learn to distinguish between general discontent and specific problems. Invest in training your employees to be "amateur" detectives. Teach them to separate problems and treat each problem with the degree of intensity it warrants. Don't use a sledgehammer to kill a gnat.

4

Can the Customer Be Satisfied?

Not every customer is going to be satisfied. Despite your best efforts, and the best writing of the world's best businesspeople, there will be a certain sector of customers who cannot be made happy. There is something you can do to make them go away and at least not harbor great resentment in their hearts toward you or your company. As we consider the options open at this point, remember that the underlying purpose in customer crisis resolution is to bring about a solution to what may at times seem like an unsolvable problem.

Act with Dispatch

Consider this: every problem will be dealt with, even those which are ignored. Just as all prayers are answered (even those which receive a "no"), all customer complaints are resolved one way or another. The fact is, however, that a problem resolved to the benefit of the company while ignoring the well-being of the consumer, has been handled badly. I simply cannot stress how important it is to consider your customer's standpoint with at least an equal standing to your own. You company does not win in any dispute that leaves the customer unhappy. Legally, and ethically, you may be in the clear. Fine. But that doesn't mean you won. Quite the contrary you always lose when the customer leaves in less than a happy frame of mind.

Children are often told they must finish some item they find on their dinner plate. Clearly, you can force most children to eat their spinach, but assuredly, you can't make them enjoy it. Likewise, you can force a resolution down a customer's throat, but just as predictablly, he or she will not enjoy it, and the result will likely be a true and deep resentment toward the company, fostered by an unyielding attitude on the part of an employee. Now, there is a way to get kids to eat their spinach without too much pain. You promise a sweet desert if they eat their greens.

The same approach works with customers' complaints. But before you can sprinkle the sugar, you must be willing to at least have the spinach served! Do not, under any circumstances allow your customer to feel that you are reluctant to help with a problem. And do not exhibit the least bit of hesitation in listening to a customer recite the litany of a complaint. Determine immediately whether or not the problem lies within the realm of your ability to correct it, and then act.

If the problem presented to you is within the scope of your influence, set about to immediately resolve it. If it turns out to be outside your sphere of expertise, than make sure the customer does not feel you are merely shoving her off to someone else. Putting your customer on a back burner, or worse, no burner at all, will only serve to reinforce her growing belief that you are less than concerned about her welfare, and more concerned about a dollar and cents transaction.

Let's visit our friend at Sell-More department store.

Scenario # 5

"So you're sure you bought these shoes here?"

"Of course I'm sure. Do you think I'm an idiot?" (answer that one rather quickly.)

"Oh, no sir! Sometimes people get confused about where they buy things, that's all."

"Well, will you replace the shoes?"

At this point the customer is asking a direct question. Now is the moment of truth. If you have the authority to make these shoes good, it is incumbent on you to do so quickly. If you don't have the authority, then you must state that fact right now. Instruct your employees to recognize questions of this sort and to act on them immediately. Do not, under any circumstances patronize your your customer. Determine what course is open to you and act on it. Act and you accomplish much; hesitate and you look like an idiot.

Offer a Satisfactory Resolution

If it is within the province of your employee to resolve the customer's complaint, then upon determining the problem is indeed legitimate, he or she must now offer a resolution. The resolution may be in the form of a refund, a replacement, or in some cases, a refund-in-kind.

The importance of offering to do whatever is needed is often blurred by management's propensity toward conservation when it comes to distribution of the company's inventory and cash. This is not the time to minimize your outlay, but rather the time to maximize on your opportunity to impress your customer with your company's sincere desire to make the buyer happy.

Consider the gentleman who decided to eat dinner at a pizza restaurant one evening. The service was slow, the pizza was cold by the time it got to his table, and to make matters worse, the waiter couldn't manage to get the drink order and dinner to arrive together. Needless to say, the patron was not a happy camper, and when he went to the cashier to pay his ticket, he was rather verbal in his grumblings. The cashier was alert to the fact that this was a dissatisfied customer, and immediately called over the manager. Moe, the manager, introduced himself and asked the deadly question: Was everything all right?

Scenario # 6

"No, everything was not all right. That was the worst service I've ever encountered in any pizza parlor anywhere in America."

"I'm really sorry that happened, sir. It's our goal to make dining here a pleasant experience."

"Well, then, you're gonna have to find some better waiters. The ones you've got couldn't be less responsive if they were comatose!"

"Please accept my apologies, and let me buy your dinner tonight."

"You don't have to do that. I understand how it is. It's not your fault."

"It's my pleasure. Your money's no good here tonight, and I hope you'll give us another chance to serve you, and next time, you'll see how we normally treat our patrons."

You'll notice how quickly the complaintant's attitude changed as soon as the manager showed how concerned he was about the problem. This is invariably the response the customer will display when he is suddenly confronted with a member of management who makes a generous effort to settle a problem. What other gestures could Moe have made? He could have offered a discount on tonight's meal. He could have knocked off a couple of dollars from the check. He might have given the guy a coupon worth one free pizza when you buy eight. Or he might have simply apologized, shrugged his shoulders, and walked off.

But the overwhelming concern exhibited to the customer told the diner one thing loud and clear. He cared! As for the customer, he'll be back because he knows Moe cares if he has a good meal or not. Proof? Moe wouldn't take his money for bad service. It's obvious Moe couldn't stay in business if he gave away free meals, and it's just as obvious it was indeed a fluke that the service was this bad. Where will the diner chose to eat next time? Why would he take a chance on going some place where the service may be slow? After all, at Moe's place the service is usually quite good!

In this case anything less than what Moe did would have been inadequate. Discounts, coupons, or indifference is not the way to run a business when it comes to the customer in crisis. Remember Moe only lost the cost of the dinner, not the retail amount. What was a fifteen dollar gift to the hapless customer was in reality only a few dollars to Moe. And in most cases Moe would gladly have given a half-price coupon to get someone in his store. He'll get the guy back in again, because the customer will always remember Moe's commitment to quality and service.

What to Do If an Offer Is Refused

There are times when the customer refuses to be satisfied. Usually in these cases the problem lies more with the elements of pride or hurt feelings. These are not common incidents, but as a customer relations expert, they are hard to accept. When a customer stands at your register and complains to the cashier that he had a terribly hard time finding an item, for example a bottle of ink, and he is berating the cashier for something the cashier clearly had no control over, you may well have a prime example of a customer that will not be satisfied.

And it may be that there is no need to try in the first place. It's possible the customer is having a bad day, predicated not on you or your store, and is merely venting his or her frustration on the first warm body he or she encounters. I've done this myself. I was unable to find Rolodex replacement cards in a business supply super store. As I was standing in the check-out line, I was a bit vocal in my critique of the store's lack of floor help. The manager of the store came over and asked what I had been looking for, and I told her. In fact, I told her everything I didn't like about her store, including the fact that the checkout lanes were too narrow.

After dumping my entire day's frustrations on this poor woman, I felt better. Foolish, but better. There was really nothing she could do or say that would have calmed me down, because the reality of the situation was that I wasn't truly all that mad at her or the store. I was angry about other things, and took it out on her. She was a wise woman. Instead of confronting me with logic or pointing out that there was a sign hanging over one aisle clearly stating "Rolodex Supplies," she instead simply said, "I'm really sorry you had that problem, sir."

Well, that was that. She was "really sorry," and I felt like an idiot. I go back there whenever I need supplies and from time to time I see the same manager. And she never fails to ask me, "Find everything okay?" I was beyond making calm that day, and certainly, she handled the situation well.

In Parting . . .

Disenchanted customers can be satisfied if the company acts with speed and dispatch. As customer problem resolution experts, we must be prepared to offer a dissatisfied customer not only a reasonable solution, but we must be prepared in the event the customer rejects our offer of compromise and be ready to determine what other course of action is available to us.

5

Determining the Origin of the Problem

Perhaps as important as knowing how to resolve a customer complaint is knowing how to prevent one in the first place. Most customer relation problems have their root in a communication breakdown. The failure to communicate can occur anywhere in the customer/store interface. To prevent communication failures, it is absolutely imperative the company find and repair potential problem areas.

Advertising as the Culprit

Advertising today is much more of a precise science than ever before. Legislation that brought about a greater awareness of "truth in advertising" also created an obligation on the part of the public to be more cognizant of what commercials offer. Unfortunately, many consumers never read the fine print, and as a result failed expectations abound.

The most obvious place to catch potential problems and stop them before they develop is in the advertising room. It is incumbent advertisers be sure their advertising is both correct and practical. The major challenge facing an advertiser is to make that item or service appear to intrinsically have more value than the price placed upon it. A sale must contain the elements of time, value, and perceived need. If in the store's zeal to present an item or service as being one of extreme urgency or need, it follows that occasionally the store will exaggerate the benefits, or at least minimize the weaknesses of their product.

When the consumer becomes the owner or user of the advertised product, and when that product fails to live up to its advertised worth, the customer understandably becomes irritated and that irritation can easily lead to a confrontation between the store and the customer. Moreover, this confrontation sets the stage for failure because the customer is entering the arena already convinced management is willing to go to any length, including publishing a lie, to attain its goal, i.e., the separation of the customer from his or her money.

Many times after a complaint arises, the company is often a victim of its own press when the customer brings in a newspaper ad that overstates either product ability or company liability. For example, the customer brings in a newspaper ad that claims the price quoted for a 21-inch color television is the lowest in a three-county area. Moreover the advertisement goes on to claim that if a lower price is found on a comparable model, the difference between the two will be doubled and given to the buyer. The key word here, of course, is "comparable." Since the chain is the only dealer of this particular "house" brand, they alone are in a position to ascertain whether or not other televisions are indeed "comparable."

This is a no-win situation. The store will do all it can to keep from making a double refund, while the customer must now take the posture of a detective searching out the error of the store's advertising. They are coming at each other in an adversarial way, both bringing a good amount of animosity to the table.

This didn't have to happen. Watch the advertisements your company makes. Don't sacrifice truth for sales. A sale made under a false assumption or pretense is in effect nothing more than a time bomb waiting to explode. On the other hand, it is not feasible to place every disclaimer, every warning, every shortcoming of the product into a printed ad. It is imperative that a balance be struck between accuracy and attraction. This is done best by the candid use of disclaimers, and rejection of any claims that may lead to disputes. Avoid such phrases as, "none better," or "lowest prices ever," or "we will not be undersold."

Customer Education

Often the root of a customer complaint is found in a basic lack of understanding about what the product is really expected to do. This is seen particularly in mechanical and electronic devices. It is important the buyer fully understand how to operate a new purchase, and how to gain the maximum benefit from all its features. Equally important, however, is that the buyer not leave the store with unrealistic expectations concerning just what the newly acquired possession will do.

Going back to Ernest Ernie's, and once again to the battery display, we see several grades of batteries, ranging from "ordinary" strength, regular carbon type, to "supreme" strength, the alkaline battery. Each battery has its selling points, but in the final analysis that selling point is longevity verses price. The cheaper the battery, the shorter its life span. Pretty basic stuff. A customer who opts to buy two "C" cell batteries for seventy-nine cents should not expect the pair to last as long as the ones for which he or she pays two-and-a-half dollars.

It is obvious the more expensive pair will last longer. What is not obvious is whether they will last three times longer, as the price would seem to indicate. Battery usage is an incredibly individual thing. Two sets of the same battery, manufactured at the same time and put into use at the same time, may vary in length of service by as much as 10 to 15 percent. Factors such as temperature, load of resistance, and even time of day will cause a battery to expend its power at a different rate of speed.

Many times, especially in today's mass merchandise outlets, there is simply no way to explain all the intricacies of a particular product to the customer as he or she ponders over which one to select. But there is a way to circumnavigate this problem. With the use of product information cards, or leaflets if practical, your company can educate its customers to the features and benefits of various products. This is especially useful when dealing with items sold in large quantities and consumed rapidly; batteries, photographic film, and light bulbs are excellent examples of the type of product that can result in an unhappy customer feeling he or she was cheated, when in reality the problem stems not from faulty products, but unrealistic expectations.

When purchasing a garment, it is customary to find washing or cleaning instructions attached to both the outer garment in the form of a hanging tag, ("Machine Washable" or "Dry

Clean Only" or "Wash in Warm Water Only") and sewn inside the garment next to the manufacturer's tag. By clearly educating the consumer, the manufacturer has taken a giant step forward toward resolving potential complaints and resentments. I recently washed a vest sweater by mistake. When I retrieved it from the dryer, I was surprised to see it had shrunk to a size four from its original extra large. I couldn't fault anyone, however, because on the tag, right next to the manufacturer's name, was a simple little three-word message: Dry Clean Only.

The sweater now adorns our dog's bed, but I would never consider blaming the store or the manufacturer for the condition of a thirty-five dollar garment now used as a dog pillow. Clearly, if the sweater had not carried that warning, I might have returned it to the store and explained that after merely one washing the item was rendered unusable. But even the most unreasonable of customers would be hard pressed to make such a claim with the instructions for cleaning so evident, and the root of the problem so clear.

Not every item can display a complete instruction manual. Products of a more technical nature require greater customer education to assure the customer will reap maximum benefits while not creating a situation that will result in the product becoming prematurely defective. While it is sufficient to limit garment cleaning instructions to simple three- or four-word sentences ("hand wash only" or "wash in warm water") items such as computers or video recording machines will often require much more detailed and complicated instructions to prevent the use of software or accessories which may injure or completely render the machines defective.

Home audio component units are complicated items. Usually they come individually boxed, each component packaged with its own instruction book, its own wiring harnesses, and its own power supply. An extremely large system may have nine to eleven components, which must work in tandem before sound will be produced. While it is true that all that's required to make the unit function is the plugging in of audio jacks connecting one component to the next, it is amazing how many consumers simply cannot follow the instructions included in each box. The problem can, however, be mitigated by providing a little guidance when the unit is sold. A tremendous number of problems can be avoided with such simple advice as "always connect the red terminals to other red terminals," or "never use a wire that is frayed, or partially exposed through the insulation."

If your customer can be made to understand some of the more intricate aspects of assembly, the odds are greatly reduced that he or she will make costly mistakes, mistakes that result in them being back in your store, holding a (now) defective stereo component and demanding a replacement or worse, a refund.

Demonstrations are an excellent way to eliminate potential customer problems. Do not assume that merely because the consumer found his or her way into your store unaided, and purchased an item such as a computer or a riding lawn mower that he or she knows how the products are to be used. There are three ways to overcome this problem. Demonstrate. Demonstrate. Demonstrate! Show the customer how to lower the amount of water the washer will require for small loads. Show him or her how to set the dial on a dryer to dry perma-press items. Demonstrate how to adjust the wheels on the vacuum cleaner for the different types of carpets, how and when to change the bags when they get full.

Five extra minutes spent with a customer explaining the intricacies of their new purchase can easily save your staff hours of paperwork and nonproductive time spent explaining that the fault lies not in the product or your store, but rather in the customer's improper installation or improper use of the product. This is time well spent, and if properly done will have the side benefit of creating good will toward both the salesperson and the store. Your customer will tell his or her friends about the "nice salesperson" who, after the sale was completed and the money already in the register took his or her time to explain a few things that really made a difference when the customer got home with the new product.

In the next segment of this chapter, we will discuss the art of troubleshooting in advance of a problem. But for now, remember one truth: **An educated customer is a more reasonable customer.**

Educating the Staff

The most dangerous and problematic aspect of any sales or service organization is an employee with the attitude "That's not my department!" A recent trend in employment has been to "cross-train" workers. This is done for two reasons. First, workers can perform more than one job and therefore be of more use to the employer. But there is a second aspect of cross-training which is singularly rewarding enough to make the concept almost a mandatory approach to modern business. The more each employee knows about the other employee's job description and expertise, the better that employee will be at handling problems that arise on a day-to-day basis.

One of the businesses in which I had an interest sold and rented furniture. I recently phoned a manufacturer's representative who calls on our firm with a question concerning the composition of the wood used to manufacture a dining room table he sold us. The sales representative who handles my account was not available, nor were there any other salespeople in the office. I told the woman who had taken my call that I had a question concerning a product her company sold, and asked her to have him call me as soon as possible. After she'd taken all the information he'd need to call me back, she said something that took me by surprise. "What's the question you need answered? Maybe I can help."

"You don't happen to know the type of wood used in a model ND 1041, do you?"

"That's the Northdrake series?"

"Yes."

"German Oak. All the Northdrake series use German Oak."

It was not until later in the day that the full impact of what she'd said hit me. This woman was not in sales. She was indeed the receptionist, the woman who answered the phone and took messages. Why then did she know the answer to a question that while not extremely technical in nature, was nonetheless asked only in trade terminology and referenced only by model number? I wanted to know more. Calling the firm the next day, I spoke to one of the owners of the company.

It was then I learned the receptionist's response was not a matter of luck, but rather a reflection of the fact that all personnel within the company, starting with the stock room workers and going right up to the president, are required to sit in on all sales meetings and new product information sessions. Moreover, all sales literature is circulated throughout the company, and each employee is expected to sign off on each piece of literature. The result of this type of involvement is incredible! Each employee has more than a passing knowledge of what's going on inside the firm, and as a result each employee is in the position of being a customer service representative.

The sales representative returned my call. Again, service! I was impressed with the fact that this company cared enough about my business to be sure their employees make a reasonable attempt to satisfy my needs. Employee education can go a long way toward heading off potential complaints and in many cases result in additional sales. Because I was able to get the answer I needed so quickly, I was able to make a sale, which of course resulted in the rep firm making an additional sale to me. After all, I needed another dining room set to replace the one I'd sold.

Troubleshooting has such a negative connotation. The troubleshooter doesn't come in until the problem exists, and then operates within an existing situation, attendant with angry customers and bewildered employees. Troubleshooting doesn't have to occur after the fact. A good portion of it could be done before trouble arrives.

We have all heard about the person who calls the service department of an appliance store to complain the refrigerator won't work, only to have a service technician come out and find it unplugged. The same is true of televisions, stereos, almost any item requiring an outside power source. I've witnessed people bring lawn mowers into service areas because the mower wouldn't start, only to find the machine was devoid of fuel or the spark plug was disconnected. Beyond the fact that such events make the customer look foolish is the obvious waste of productive time such occurences cause the company, particularly in situations in which some sort of warranty is in place.

Again, employee education could and would solve many of these false alarms. If the person taking the call from the customer whose refrigerator would not run had asked, in a polite and kind manner, "You have checked to be sure it's plugged in, haven't you?" the whole affair could have been managed in just a few minutes, instead of sending a man and a truck 20 miles across town to plug it in himself.

Years ago I sold a customer in Denver a shipment of NFL clocks. These clocks were housed in molded plastic made to resemble a football helmet, and each helmet had the markings of a different NFL team. They were great sellers, and this particular customer purchased one hundred dozen clocks. Five days later he was on the phone to me, very disturbed. He told me none of the clocks worked. Not one out of twelve hundred. Not one!

I was mortified. Beyond the fact that I had an unhappy customer on the phone was the fact that I still had well over fifteen hundred dozen of those clocks in my warehouse and at least that many already shipped to other customers. I mentally ran down the list of what could have been wrong. I asked him if he had tried one himself. He replied that he'd tried 36 of them, and not one had worked. I asked him if he'd tried plugging them into different outlets. He said he had plugged them into outlets that were running other electrical items, so he knew the outlets were hot. Finally, I told him I'd call him right back, and went out to the warehouse to get a sample to look at myself.

I called him back, this time with my sample in hand, and went through the procedure for setting the clock itself. I asked him to go step by step with me. Over the phone we both took a clock out of the box, we both unwraped the plastic seal around it, both reached down to plug it into an outlet. I then pulled off the blackout tape that displayed a permanent "12:00," and proceeded to set my clock, which was working fine. My customer, however, stopped me when he asked, "What blackout tape?"

"The one covering where the L.E.D. display will read out the correct time."

There was silence on the other end for about 10 seconds. And in those 10 seconds, I realized, as did my customer, that he had omitted the most fundamental part of setting the clock. He had failed to remove the tape from the L.E.D. window. All the clocks he saw said 12:00, even when they were not plugged in. I wanted to laugh, but one doesn't laugh at a customer, especially one of his magnitude. Instead I only said, "Well, Al, things like that happen. Tricky little buggers, aren't they?"

While it is true I didn't lose the sale, I did spend 15 very worried minutes thinking about buying back eleven thousand dollars worth of inventory, not to mention the loss I would have suffered if the entire inventory had been defective. Could I have foreseen such a problem? Probably not. Did I correct it in the future? Bet the farm! I put out a memo to all salespeople, as well as our technical staff, and our receptionists, alerting them to the potential problem that existed with this product, and the attendant remedy. In the next four weeks, we fielded questions from 19 different customers about the L.E.D. window cover, and each time, our people were able to handle the problem quickly and with a minimum of time expended.

Never underestimate the lack of expertise your customer brings to the table with a new item. We had taken the problem of the tape cover for granted. It was even commented on when we evaluated the product because it gave the clock such an appealing look while on display. It never occurred to me or any of my staff that the very sticker we liked so much would in effect become a detriment to our selling the product.

An employee not involved in problem solving is an employee involved in problem making. There should be no one in your employ who does not understand the basic concept of customer service. I've heard secretaries say they were "only" secretaries, and not involved in the sales department. Wrong! There is not a single employee at General Motors, or at IBM not involved in sales. From the guy who sweeps the floor to the account executive who signs the order, every employee in your firm is a customer service representative. If you fail to impress that on them, you are not maximizing your service efforts.

Moreover, if you have an employee who refuses to understand his or her part in customer service, you are shooting yourself in the foot by keeping them in your employ.

In order to insure all your workers are service oriented, include them in sales seminars, and provide them with ongoing product knowledge and customer awareness. Involve everyone. If employees see that customer service is indeed important to you, it will become important to them. Why do all your employees show up for work at their appointed times? Because you insist on it. Why do they all dress according to your company's code? Because you have made it part of their job description. How do you get them all involved in customer service? You tell them they must be.

There are many ways you can encourage your workers to be more service oriented. Have monthly meetings for the sole purpose of recognizing those employees who have done something above and beyond the call of duty. Present a plaque of some sort to commemorate the occasion. Perhaps reward that worker with a savings bond, or an afternoon off, or a prized parking spot for the month. The reward doesn't have to bankrupt your company, but it must be significant. If customer service is a worthwhile goal, then achieving a higher level of service must be worth the employee's effort. Remember, a smile and a kind word is nice, but a smile and a kind word and twenty-five dollars is much nicer!

Vendor Cooperation in Quality Control

Walmart is unquestionably one of America's most outstanding examples of retail growth. Their basis for growth, to a certain extent, rests on their ability to retail merchandise at a lower cost than their competitors. This is accomplished a number of different ways; volume buying is one, but even more effective is the way they buy. When Walmart takes on a new vendor, that vendor becomes responsible for defective merchandise in a way never before done. Walmart actually charges the vendor to handle defects, above and beyond the traditional charge back of the cost of the goods. This encourages vendors to only send their first-line merchandise to Walmart stores. The practice has two benefits. First, while customers may not be aware of this buying practice, they soon become aware of the results, i.e., fewer products purchased containing manufacturer's defects, and second, because vendors tend to send only first-line merchandise to Walmart, Walmart in turn does not waste a lot of its time handling returns and unhappy customers.

It is obvious that most retail vendors do not have the buying clout of Walmart or Sears. This does not mean, however, that they must accept faulty or shabby merchandise from their vendors. Offering quality merchandise begins in the buyer's offices. Over the last 20 years, I have begun all buying relations with manufacturer's representatives by showing them my defect record book. I explain to them that every defect is recorded in the book, and a copy of the report is placed in the vendor's file. When the time comes to reorder, one of the first considerations of any of my companies is the defect rate. We impress on the vendor the fact that a high defect rate will not only cost them the item they are selling us, but any other lines we carry that they sell.

Heavy handed? Perhaps. Effective? Extremely!

We are not in business to handle other company's problems or defects. Some manufacturer's defects are understandable, even expected. But excessive defects are the seedlings from which giant problems grow, and your company simply should refuse to participate in any merchandising program which fosters a high rate of returns. In essence, what must be done is to put the onus of returns back on the vendor, not on your customers or your salespeople. Your customers don't deserve it, and your employees don't have time for it.

In Parting . . .

When determining the origin of a customer service problem, don't overlook the possibility that the problem had its roots in the claims and assertions made by your advertising department. Work toward bringing your media statements in line with reality, try not to promise benefits and services that your company cannot provide. Allow your advertising department to function not only as a propaganda device, but also as a dissemination center to teach your customers, and your staff, about the advantages and limitations of any product or service your company offers.

6

Writing Resolution Reports: The Need for Complete and Accurate Records

Over the course of several months and quarters, it becomes increasingly difficult to remember the nature, time frame, and remedy of past problems. There is a natural inclination among the best of us to remember bad times as worse than they were, and good times as better than they could possibly have been.

Without complete and accurate records, problem areas cannot be clearly identified, nor can time frames be properly drawn. An example of a correctly documented problem resolution report is given in Chapter 3. Keep in mind that for the report to be of any use whatsoever, it must be fully filled in, including dates, product brands and model numbers, names of personnel involved, and the nature of the complaint, as well as the resolution.

No one likes more paperwork, and this method certainly does involve more but trying to maintain a customer resolution team without proper documentation is really an exercise in futility. Moreover, once your resolution team becomes comfortable with the structure of the forms, they will become second nature.

The Strength of a Written Report versus a Verbal Report

As suggested in Chapter 3, the forms should be kept in triplicate. One copy should be maintained in a three-ring binder, sorted by vendor or manufacturer. The second should be placed in a file, chronologically sorted, and the third should be circulated during customer resolution team meetings. Meetings should be scheduled frequently enough to insure problem patterns can be quickly discerned before the problems have a chance to root themselves in your organization, but not so frequently as to diminish the value of the service meetings. Meetings held too often tend to become rote, and the topic being discussed can be relegated to the position of nuisance rather than high priority.

By maintaining written reports, your company can more easily track defective merchandise as it is outbound, after causing trouble, and hopefully stop such items as they are inbound, before trouble can occur.

One of my companies repeatedly tried to market outdoor amplifiers that would increase the signal sent from an outside television antenna to the television receiver inside the house. We purchased the units from three different vendors. All three units were manufactured in Asia, and all three looked the same; the only difference was the lot identification number.

We determined we were having a failure rate of almost 50 percent of all units sold. After separating the three vendors into separate categories for the purpose of quality control, we learned that one vendor had a defect rate of almost 80 percent, another a defect rate of 85 percent. But the third vendor had a defect rate of less than 22 percent. As a group, one out of two amplifiers were failing. But when we eliminated the first two vendors, our defect rate dropped to 22 percent!

Without proper paperwork we might never have focused on the root of the defect rate on this item.

Reinforcement of Company Policy

The second reason for proper documentation is a bit more obscure, yet equally as viable as the others. With each documentation of a customer's complaint, the employee handling the problem receives an extra reminder about how important customer service is to your company. Through repetition we learn. And through constant use of written problem resolution reports, each employee participating in the program is reminded of your company's commitment to perfect customer satisfaction.

In addition to reinforcement of company policy, a company that maintains complete records of all customer disputes can often call upon these records to defend themselves, (should the need ever arise) in a court of law. Each document serves as a memorandum to the file, and as such, in most states, each is admissible in court. The very fact that your company keeps such detailed records of the way it conducts business could in effect become a means of defense against a lawsuit claiming willful negligence or careless conduct. It would be foolish to accuse any entity of negligence when it is obvious that entity is extremely sensitive to customer problems.

Reports as Training Tools

Each occurrence of a customer complaint is a learning opportunity as well as an opportunity to show your customers how much you value their business. To that end, it is vitally important your workers take time to fill out the resolution report in as detailed a way as possible. This form is more than just a record of a defective piece of merchandise or a service gone awry. This form is the heartbeat of the offended or aggrieved customer. It is vitally important the customer not get the feeling he or she is merely answering useless questions as a way for the store to "get even" with the customer for bringing the problem to the attention of management. Indeed, the customer should be made to feel that he or she is an integral part of a much bigger problem and a key element in the solution of that problem.

Every time your employee fills out a report, he or she should be thinking of methods and means to prevent its reoccurrence. From that standpoint alone, it is worth the effort to fully document each problem and its resolution.

Be sure to encourage your problem resolution team to try innovative approaches to problem solving. Once they are assured of company support, the ingenuity a resourceful problem resolver can bring to the table is amazing. One member of a problem resolution team in a St. Louis electronics super store came up with the "Hook-Up Hot Line." This concept, which was really nothing more than a series of three-minute audio tapes, allowed customers to call a special telephone number, hit a few keys on the touch pad, and hear a recorded message that would help them hook up their stereos, video cassette recorders, or home component systems; it even worked for computer installations. This system was designed after the aforementioned employee had filled out his fifth problem resolution form stemming from the improper hookup of a video cassette recorder.

Establishing a Livable Procedure

No single style of customer relations or service will fit every business. Just as you cannot hope to make everyone happy with one policy in any other respect, you will not make everyone happy with your problem resolution team. But this is no reason not to try. There are certain parameters which must be observed, and by doing so, the chances for success with your program will be greatly enhanced.

Procedures in Relation to Industry Standards

In the field of customer relations, it should be the goal of your company to lead your industry with new and resourceful programs. Before this can be done, however, you must know what the standards of your industry are. In the tire industry, for example, it is customary to replace defective tires predicated on tread wear, that is, to prorate the usable life of a tire predicated on how much tread is left on the tire when an irreparable injury occurs. This warranty is a pretty cut and dried proposition, and requires very little problem solving on the part of the adjuster.

In the auto industry there is little question about what is covered by warranty and what is not, or about length of coverage in relation to mileage and time. Most new cars carry a fifty thousand mile or five-year warranty, whichever comes first. If, therefore, you were to design a new car, and your aim was to be competitive in the market place, your new product would carry at least the same warranty as the other models already on the market. This is a classic example of industry standards setting the policies for all companies within a certain industry.

Industry standards, however, were made to be exceeded. They tend to be conservative in nature, and are as regressive as the industry will allow them to be. Going back to the tire warranty, it should be remembered that at one time all tires were sold without warranty in regard to road hazards. Later, as competition increased, various companies ventured into the world of road hazard warranties. Obviously, it cannot be the manufacturer's fault if a driver runs over a bottle, a nail, or a piece of metal and tears the fabric of the tire. Nonetheless, in the sixties and seventies, most tire companies offered a warranty that included a standard "road hazard" warranty.

Soon all tire manufacturers were offering a road hazard warranty. And as the decade of the seventies wore on, it became obvious that loses were being incurred through no fault of the manufacturer. The difficult aspect of the warranty was that nothing could be done to limit the liability the manufacturer faced. Theoretically, every tire sold was a potential warranty candidate. As a practical matter, tire companies started to either eliminate the road hazard warranty, or severally restrict it by making prorating a more obscure art, predicated to a large extent on a concept of "predetermining" the amount of compensation allowed. Some companies began the practice of selling a road hazard warranty as an add-on sale, more of an insurance policy than a legitimate warranty.

As the industry adjusted to this concept, and even warmed to it, competition reared its ugly head once more, and soon some companies were once more offering a limited road hazard warranty. Now it is not unusual to see road hazard as a standard selling point when one visits a tire store. This is a classic example of the individual members of an industry allowing their policy to be set by industry standards. The basic problem with this concept, of course, is that most companies are forever playing catch-up with the competition. They are never in the position of being a leader, but rather continually find themselves reacting to the competition. Thinking like this is what leads to price wars and blown-out markets.

Procedures in Relation to Regional Expectations

Setting your customer service resolution policy to the expectations of your particular region has several pitfalls. It is a given that people in the northeastern section of the United States tend to expect a lower level of service than their counterpart in the Southwest; but many retail operations are national or even international in scope. From a purely practical standpoint, it is not reasonable, nor is it good business to try to design a customer service resolution team's activities based on regional considerations. It follows then, that one would not expect to tell their managers they should replace defective light bulbs for disgruntled customers in Austin, while telling customers in Boston with the same problem that there is nothing the company can do.

What happens when the manager of the Boston store gets transferred to Austin? How many customers will she lose for the company before she gets a handle on the regional differences between the two cities? Obviously this approach won't wash with a national company, and moreover, it flies in the face of customer problem resolution. Consistency is the pearl of this situation. Your company's policy toward handling defective light bulbs in Boston should be the same as in Austin. Anything else is shortchanging not only your customer but your company.

Procedures in Relation to Vendors

Perhaps the worst possible measure to use in determining what your policies will be in regard to customer service problems is the service policy of your vendors. We studied the problem of the hapless customer who purchased batteries for his portable stereo only to arrive home and find them defective. As noted earlier, batteries tend not to show any wear, regardless of how old they are. It is virtually impossible to differentiate between a fresh battery and one taken from an appliance after all its energy has been depleted. Because of this, the battery industry maintains very rigid policies concerning defective and returned merchandise.

With this restrictive policy in mind, most companies that retail batteries are hesitant to accept back for warranty any batteries for any reason. What this means is companies are forced to either adhere to the rules of their vendor in regard to a warranty policy or be prepared to suffer the financial loss themselves when they find themselves without recourse after making a warranty decision contrary to the stated policy of the vendor or manufacturer.

In essence, a policy of setting warranties to accommodate your vendor results in taking away from your company the initiative in dealing with customer problems and placing the authority (and growth) of your policies in another company's hands. How dangerous this could be! You would not consider for a moment relinquishing your autonomy to an advertising firm, or an accounting firm. But without a whimper many companies literally stand back and allow a stranger, whose interests, by the way, do not always coincide with theirs, to run an integral part of your business, that of customer relations.

There is an up side to this situation, however. As in the case of Walmart, it is possible for a company to force its vendors to agree to their form of customer service. If it is the policy of your company to refund batteries brought back to your store with claims of product defectiveness, than that policy should be explained to the vendor who wishes to sell your company batteries. If they want your business badly enough, they will make the necessary changes in their policy. If, on the other hand, they remain rigid and inflexible, your purchase order should remain in the drawer. In today's economy there is always someone standing in the wings, waiting to supply your needs. That someone may well be amenable to playing ball under your rules.

I once owned a company involved in the distribution of car audio equipment. Because we sold our products across the nation, via telemarketing, it was important that our warranty policy be quite flexible. A problem we encountered continually was how to handle defective stereos that had been installed in an automobile. Clearly, because most of our customers were in other states, it would not be practical for them to remove the stereo from the auto, ship it back to us, wait 10 days to three weeks for us to repair and reship the same unit back to the customer, and then reinstall the unit.

But just as clearly, we could not afford to replace the stereo with a new unit, and take the old one back in for repairs. The result of such a strategy would have been to turn our inventory of new audio equipment into an inventory of used junk rather quickly. If we were to continue handling these products, we knew a more flexible solution to the problem would have to be found. We also knew the only way this would ever work was to negotiate a special arrangement with our vendors.

In the end, our solution was quite simple. Before we would purchase any line of car stereos, the vendor wishing to sell to us would agree to an "over-the-counter" warranty. This meant when one of our dealers was faced with a defective unit, the dealer would simply pull the bad unit from the customer's auto, replace it with a new one, and ship the old unit back to us in the box from which the new unit was taken. We would issue our customer a new unit, and the factory from which we purchased the stereo would likewise credit us with a new radio. The problem of disposing of used radios became my vendor's headache, not mine.

Obviously, our solution placed us in a strong marketing position because our over-the-counter warranty made life so much easier for our customers that they favored our firm with more business. The very thing that should have kept us from doing business with companies halfway across America was the thing we turned into a strength. But left to the mercy of our vendors, we would have never built the momentum we needed to become a national distributor.

Procedures in Relation to Customer Expectations

If vendors are the worst yardsticks by which to measure and determine what your customer service policies should be, it follows that your customer's expectations are the best and most valid considerations when finally setting a policy statement that will guide your employees as they make their way through a very difficult aspect of business.

As stated earlier, one of the keys to dealing with an irate customer is to treat him as he would want to be treated, not as *you* want to be treated. Following that concept to its logical conclusion, it should therefore be your company's goal to fashion its policies on the expectations of its customers. Life is not complicated, nor is customer service. Most of us want the same thing. When we pay for a product, we want that product to work, and work in as problem-free a manner as possible. That's it. We don't buy manufacturer's defects, we don't buy obsolete technology, we don't buy problems, back orders, or unclear instructions. We buy things we need, or want, and we expect those things to work.

Anything that comes between us and the utility of the product or service we have bought needs to be minimized. Anything that enhances our enjoyment of those goods or services needs to be maximized. Set your company's service policies toward that goal, and you will outdistance the nearest competitor by light years. Fail to do it, and your company will always be an "also ran."

In Parting . . .

Writing a report every time your company deals with a defective piece of merchandise or a service problem may seem like an awful lot of excessive paperwork. Only by keeping a written journal, however, can you hope to maintain the proper records and track not only existing problems, but forecast with a certain degree of accuracy future problems and danger areas.

7

Answering the Bell

Unfortunately, not all customer complaints will be presented in person. A percentage of your disgruntled customers will employ the telephone to convey their dissatisfaction with your products or your employees. It should be realized that of all the mediums that your customer can choose to lodge complaints, the telephone is the most likely to result in a further tangling of the situation, rather than a satisfactory resolution.

Telephones are by nature a most restrictive mode of communication. There are several reasons for this; the most obvious is that telephones do not allow for any transference of information that might otherwise be gained by the observation and interpretation of body language. Psychologists rely heavily on how a person uses his or her body for communications. In many cases, how a person holds her head, focuses her eyes, and crosses her arms or legs will reveal more about that person than what she is saying.

Clues to a person's mental condition are often revealed by body language. Telephones do not allow these clues to come through the line. Moreover, the actual mechanics of telephones and telephone calls work against a clear understanding of what the caller is trying to express. If it were not bad enough that we are deprived of the physical antics of the caller, we are now faced with the problem of sorting out what a person is saying from how a person is saying it. For example, if your crisis customer is prone to sarcasm, it will be amplified over a nonphysical presentation of a problem. Listen to how this sounds:

"Right. I can tell you're real concerned."

Sounds like the person saying this is being sarcastic, and confrontational. Now, repeat that same sentence, only this time add the physical antics of the customer raising his right hand about halfway up his body and turning it slightly upward, tilting his head a bit to the left and saying the same thing. This time, the same sentence can mean, "Wait. I know you are real concerned."

The difference here is not semantics, but body language. The crisis customer is not able to get her point across as effectively as she might if they were sitting opposite you, across a desk, or in your showroom. This is not a one-sided problem, however. Regardless of how concerned you as the resolution manager may be about her problem, your message is also hampered by a lack of visible body language. Your customer is already in an adversarial relationship by virtue of the fact she has a problem. Any lack of sincerity on your part, be it real or imagined, is magnified by a lack of visual input.

Other mechanical problems play into this situation as well. Phone lines that are not crystal clear will cause the dialogue between the two of you to be strained. In addition to being angry over her problem, the customer must now strain to either hear your response, or make her assertions clear despite the bad connection. Add to this the fact that since AT&T was broken into smaller companies, and competition was allowed into the marketplace to sell both hardware and phone lines, the general quality of phone service has suffered. At one time we were fairly confident that the equipment both we and the caller was using was of the same high quality. This is no longer the case. Telephone receivers have various degrees of clarity. It is possible that while your company has spent upwards of three hundred dollars for the phone on your desk, your crisis customer is speaking to you on a telephone she received free for buying sixteen boxes of breakfast cereal.

Environmental conditions, such as cold weather, wet lines, or even extremely hot, dry days can influence how well local and long distance lines will function. Party lines, crossed lines, busy switching centers, and equipment racked with overloaded calls on certain days (days such as the first day of summer vacation, holidays, or times of national crisis, or heavy loss days in the market), will result in phone service which is less than optimal. Your customer will feel the pressure of his inability to communicate clearly as further frustration. This frustration will do nothing but escalate his feelings of neglect and will result in his further perception that he is David fighting an unconcerned Goliath!

The telephone is no friend of the problem resolution manager. There are times, however, when a situation exists that cannot be remedied by any other means than the telephone. This is not to say that in such situations there is no recourse, it is only to point out that when the customer resolution manager must handle complaints via phone lines, caution and care must be exercised. This chapter will deal with how to best use the phone to your advantage. To do so will require a bit more patience, a bit more tact, and a good deal of organizational skill.

Establishing Telephone Policies

It is a fact of business life that sooner or later every person in your organization will eventually answer your telephone. This includes the CEO who answers the phone because it's rung 30 times and he picks it up in frustration because he cannot understand why no one else has, right down to the janitor whose total understanding of the English language is the phrase, "Can you tell me where the broom is?" This is a regrettable truth, because in all probability, neither the CEO nor the janitor has been trained in the proper handling of an irate caller.

To this end, it behooves every company, regardless of size or mission, to see that all employees are given a minimal amount of training that will at least make them cognizant of the importance of the incoming call. Remember that to the customer on the other end, whoever answers the phone is the company. All too often, the task of phone receptionist is given to a person whose job description reads like the directions found on a shampoo bottle, "Apply, rinse, apply."

How to Answer

I have been shocked to call companies whose employees have answered the phone with a simple, "Hello." Invariably, when I encounter such a greeting, I immediately doubt that I've reached the proper number. Moreover, I am put in the position of having to identify the company for the phone receptionist. Listen to this exchange.

"Hello."

"Is this the Acme Tool Company?"

"Yes, it is."

"I need to speak to someone who can help me with a problem."

"One moment, please."

And I am on hold! I am already relatively sure that I've reached the home of one of the executives by mistake, or at best, that I have been put into "hold hell" from which there is no escape. This conversation, has gone from bad to worse. Within 10 seconds, I am off the line and calling again. The only thing worse than not getting an answer is getting one which is meaningless, signifying to me that I am about to have to fight my way into the corporate morass of unconcerned employees and a lax company policy. If I was annoyed before, I am now ready for a fight! I redial.

"Acme Tool."

"Yes. I called a moment ago and asked to speak to someone who could help me with a problem."

"Please hold."

By now, I am no longer in the mood to hold, but at least I feel that I'm making some progress. That feeling evaporates 30 seconds later when the same person who first answered my call returns with what must be the most frustrating thing a telephone receptionist can say. "Who are you holding for?"

Let's stop for a moment and figure out how and where the call went awry. In the first place the person who answered my call did not identify herself. She is a faceless, nameless person. And she has succeeded in making me the same nonentity. Not only did I not know who I was holding for, but I didn't know who I was speaking to when the phone receptionist came back on the line. The receptionist had further muddied the water by placing me in a position of having to admit I didn't know with whom I needed to speak. Hardly the way to begin a call that was originated because of a lack of satisfaction in the first place.

The fact that I was placed on hold, without my consent, further added to my discontent about the way the whole affair was being handled. By the second time I'd been placed on hold, I was becoming more and more disenchanted with Acme Tool. There was a third element of this conversation that also caused me concern. How would the operator have transferred me in the first place? She didn't know the nature of my problem; she could not have directed my call with any degree of accuracy. Inevitably, I would reach a second person, who then would have had to perform triage on my situation, and only then would my call be directed to the party capable of resolving my problem.

My call should have taken an entirely different route. The telephone receptionist should have handled my call in the following manner:

"Acme Tool, this is Amy. How may I direct your call?"

"Amy, I have a problem and I need some help."

"Certainly, sir. May I ask the nature of your problem and I'll connect you with someone who can help."

See the difference? Even if the phone was ringing off the wall, how much longer would it have taken her to say, "If you could hold just a moment, I'll help you find the party you need." The significant difference here is that instead of an ominous cloud forming over my call, instead of an unknown voice shuffling me off to the great wasteland of "Hold Please" I actually was speaking to a person. I didn't know Amy from Adam's house cat, but a bond was in place, however tenuous, and I at least felt connected to a person, not a voice. When Amy returned, she would have continued the conversation by asking me the nature of my problem. Once she was able to identify the area in which my dispute arose, that is, whether I needed to be connected to the credit department, to sales, or to shipping, she could have expedited my call to the proper department.

As it happened, however, I was connected to the sales manager's secretary. Not a good guess on the receptionist's part, as my question, and problem, centered around my billing. In the end I was placed on hold three times before I was connected with the accounts receivable department. The handling of my call was not Amy's fault, however. To blame her would have been to excuse management for their sloppy job of training her in the proper exercise of phone etiquette.

The Urgency of Proper Training

Amy was unable to do her job because no one had taken the time to properly train her. Most companies give only the most cursory training to the person who's job it will be to represent their company to everyone who calls. She is not merely the "girl" who answered the phone; she *is* Acme Tool. As I've said, I didn't know her from the infamous house cat belonging to Adam. No one had told her how important a job she held, how vital the first contact with the caller really is. Had she worked for me, her entire attitude would have been different.

There are certain things any telephone receptionist absolutely must know. He or she must have a working knowledge of how the corporation functions. He or she should not only know about the different divisions within the company's framework, but should know what each division does. When a customer says he or she is having a problem with a bill, it is incumbent upon the phone receptionist to not only know that this is an accounting problem but to know that every accounting department has two divisions, accounts payable and accounts receivable. The purpose here is to allow the receptionist to direct the call to the right department on the first try. Each time a customer is placed on hold and the call is directed to another area, that customer's call is at risk. Disconnected calls, unanswered pages, or misdirected calls place the company's reputation in jeopardy. After all, would you really want to place an order with an organization that can't even get a phone call right?

As part of basic orientation, the phone receptionist should be made aware of the company's policy on how many times the phone should be allowed to ring before it's answered. We all know that no one wants to answer on the first ring; to do so conveys the image of a company that is not doing much business. That image usually goes hand in hand with a company that is not successful. But coyness only goes so far in business, and after that, the corporate image begins to suffer. The caller wonders why any company would not have adequate people on hand to at least answer a phone. If incoming phone calls can be treated with such a cavalier attitude, how much attention will be given to an order or a complaint?

Most companies that have established a limit on the number of times a phone should ring have settled on either three or four. Fewer than three exhibits an overeagerness that should be avoided. More than four indicates a company either overtaxed or uninterested in the customer's needs. The crucial thing here is that in the absence of a strict telephone policy, the customer is left to the capricious whims of an untrained receptionist. Nothing good can come from such a corporate attitude.

The Mechanics of Handling Incoming Calls

While the focus of this book is the handling of crisis customers, properly applied phone techniques can mitigate and possibly totally eliminate the need for handling crisis customers by eliminating the crisis entirely. This is a critical area, and proper training here is crucial.

Your phone receptionist should be instructed that each incoming call has three major components. The elements are the degree of urgency, the expectation of a result, and the resolution of the call. Almost without exception, all incoming calls will contain these elements.

Urgency of the Call

All incoming calls have some level of urgency. Even those calls that appear to be mundane in nature, such as inquires about hours of operation or what means of payment are acceptable for a transaction, contain this element. Consider this: if a call were totally without purpose, would the caller have placed it in the first place? Probably not. Yet all calls do not have the same level of urgency. Certainly an incoming call asking if the company accepts American Express is not on the level of one demanding to know the name of the company's president. Teach your phone receptionist to be able to differentiate between such calls.

As important as it is to train your people to disseminate information on a timely basis, it is equally important they know what information is proprietary in nature. There is a world of difference between "What time do you open?" and "Can you tell me which bank your company uses as its main depository?" Surprisingly enough, many phone receptionists will spill their guts to anyone who calls asking any question to which they are privy to the answer. I listened in horror one day as my phone receptionist related not only the name of my bank, but our account number, as well as the amount of our last deposit. I probably don't have to tell you, she's not with us anymore.

The Expectation of the Caller

When anyone calls your company, he or she usually has expectations concerning their call. Going back to the question of "What time do you open?" it is reasonable to suppose that the caller expects a simple answer. This isn't brain surgery. You open at eight in the morning. Your phone receptionist should be able to answer this question without referring it to another employee. Even incoming calls dealing with technical questions are based on the expectation the phone receptionist will be able to forward the call to the appropriate department.

The problems that will arise at the phone receptionist desk should be dealt with in one of three manners.

1. If the phone receptionist can answer the question without consulting another employee, he or she should do so.

2. If the query is beyond the scope of the phone receptionist's expertise or authority, the call should be forwarded to the appropriate department.

3. If the call is one that deals with a question or problem that falls outside the realm of normal business activity, or into a field that could possibly be handled by more than one division within the company, it is perfectly acceptable for the phone receptionist to query the caller for more information.

If, for example, the caller is asking to speak to someone about a donation to a charity, the call might be routed to either the publicity department or the treasurer's office or perhaps even to the CEO. In order to properly direct the call, the receptionist should ask the caller what type of donation they are seeking. There is considerable difference between a request for a corporate donation to help a local chapter of the PTA and a request to borrow the corporate jet to fly in a celebrity for a rally to support the building of a new hospital. And that determination will be instrumental in whether or not the caller is directed to Mr. Wilson in promotions, or Ms. Kelly in public relations.

Telephone Problem Resolution

There are only two ways a call can be resolved. The caller can either be given the requested information, or he or she can be directed to the proper division or employee. There are no other satisfactory ways to handle an incoming call.

Assuming that the incoming call could not be handled at the first level, by the phone receptionist, the call must be forwarded to another area. Your phone receptionist should never say, "Please hold; I'll connect you." Now this may seem like a contradiction in terms of what you've hired the phone receptionist to do. You have, after all, employed this person to direct calls. But the ugly specter of "Hold hell" looms over such a statement.

When your phone receptionist is about to transfer a call, she or he should first identify for the caller the name or at least the extension number of the party the caller is being transferred to. Let's listen to Amy answer the phone.

"Acme Tool. My name is Amy. How may I direct your call?"

"Ah, yes. I need to talk to someone about a problem I'm having."

"Yes, sir. Could you tell me the nature of the problem, and I'll be glad to direct your call."

"I ordered three dozen hammers, and I was billed for six dozen, but only received two dozen."

"I'm sorry you had that problem. Let me connect you with Ms. Jamerson. She's at extension 335. Could you please hold?"

"Yeah, sure."

"Thank you."

How smoothly that went! Needless to say, the last thing this customer needed was to be shuffled back and forth between the sales department, the shipping room, and accounts receivable. Amy may not have known what department to give the call to, but Ms. Jamerson, her supervisor, would. Rather rather than have the caller wait while Amy tracked down three department heads, querying all three about whose problem this was, she passed the call to her supervisor, who presumably would possess the expertise to direct this call to the proper department.

Recently I placed a call to a pizza restaurant in our city. The purpose of the call was to solicit 10 pizzas for a donation to a local middle school. My call was answered by a young man who began the conversation by saying, "Checkers Pizza, may I have your phone number?" Now I wasn't adverse to giving my phone number, but I knew this question was posed because the person on the other end thought I was placing an order. I was not. I was asking for a donation for a very worthy cause. Moreover, I knew that if I gave him my phone number, his next question would be, "And what did you want to order?" By this time, he would have already started to input my order, at which time I would have told him I didn't want to order. You see the problem here. I didn't give him my telephone number; I said instead, "I'm not calling to place an order. I need to speak to the manager."

There is something forboding about asking to speak to the manager. Obviously, it wasn't a personal call. If it were, I'd have asked to speak to Mike, or Sally, or whoever the manager happened to be. But by breaking out of the mode of most of the calls the pizzeria receives, I had put the young man on the defensive, needlessly I might add. As it turned out, he was the manager. Again, trying to be as personable as possible, (I was after all asking for 10 free pizzas) I asked a very normal question. I asked him his name. Now this wouldn't have been necessary if he'd answered the phone by saying, "Checker's Pizza. This is Chuck. May I have your phone number?"

His answer absolutely floored me. Instead of responding to my question, he asked me one in return. "Why do you want to know?" Why indeed! I was now the one on the defensive. This call was becoming a battle of wills, and in this case, I was in no position to take a superior attitude. I found myself in the unenviable position of placing my request before a person who obviously didn't trust my motives from the outset. His hostility to my innocent question about his name set the tone of the call. To my amazement, however, he did donate the pizzas. It was with considerable regret that I concluded this man was either wanted by the police or at the very least, by a hostile ex-wife. I was wrong however, and we have since become good friends. Consider this. **If the manager had such shockingly bad telephone manners, what hope did he have the rest of the crew would be any better?**

If your telephone receptionist is trained to recognize the three components of all incoming calls, the urgency of the call, the expectation and the resolution, you will notice an increase in the entire staff's productivity with regard to the handling of any problems related to telephone interaction between your staff and your customers. Not only will there be less bungled phone calls, but the overall confidence of your office staff in their ability to handle phone problems will be markedly improved

Being a Messenger

Communication is the heart of all organizations. But so many companies overlook the obvious when trying to improve the flow of information within the corporate structure. Regardless of how well information flows within your business, it will all go astray if the message center is not in step with the rest of the company.

There are as many systems for the rapid dispatch of phone messages as there are phone receptionists. Companies can literally spend a fortune on various types of "schemes" to insure all employees receive all their telephone messages. Voice mail, carbon copies of all messages, computer posting for quick reference, even the old fashioned, "stick-em" type notes (my personal favorite) pasted all over the intended recipient's phone.

Despite this quest for efficiency, there remains at the core of all incoming messages only four integral parts to any incoming message: time and date, the party called, the party calling, and the message. In the final analysis, all that really matters is that the messages reach the intended receiptient. To this end, your telephone receptionist must pass on these four elements to the proper employees.

Time and Date

Incredible as this may sound, a large number of telephone receptionists consider the time and date of an incoming message to be of little consequence. If this were a perfect world, everyone would return all their incoming phone messages before the day was over, and there would be no need to write the time and date on the message slip. I have suffered the embarrassment of calling an individual, only to find out the call I was returning was generated from a message I'd received two or three days earlier.

The practice of writing the time and date on messages will eliminate this danger. Moreover, it also results in saved expenditures, not just in long distance charges, but in increased productivity by virtue of not wasting time and effort on a call which had already been answered, or whose time frame rendered them moot. There is an intangible savings of credibility. Our business associates may laugh off the unnecessarily returned call, but the damage it does to our reputation for efficiency and accuracy leaves a debit that cannot easily be erased.

A worse-case scenario results when an employee calls a second time to resolve a problem he or she handled days ago, and the intended person for whom that employee was calling is away from his or her desk, thus creating another round of return calls, this time from the person your employee called. Telephone tag is at best an annoying game. Add to that the fact that there really was no basis for the game in the first place, and you can readily see how counterproductive such a practice can be.

One final compelling reason for accurate time keeping in the receipt of incoming messages is that failure to do so will also result in an employee's inability to substantiate the fact that he or she is on top of their responsibilities. An accurate paper trail of when a customer first called, will head off the nebulous complaint, "I've called a dozen times in the last week, and you've never returned my calls!" **It is imperative that all messages be timed and dated.**

Who Called?

Nothing is as frustrating as finding a message that reads "Jim called." I probably know 12 men named Jim. I received just such a message, but it contained the one word that got my immediate attention. "Urgent!" Right. Now I had an urgent call from an unknown business associate named "Jim" and he had an "urgent" problem. I asked the telephone receptionist "Jim who?" Her blank stare told the whole story. "Just Jim. He said you'd know who he was."

Of course, I didn't. But I knew he needed to speak to me at once. The next day he called back, irate that I'd not returned his call. Irate and irrational, I might add. I tried to explain the cryptic message I'd been given. His response? "Well, just how many Jim's do you know?"

I eventually extricated myself from this snafu, but be assured, it was not without a certain cost. My telephone receptionist looked bad, my organization looked sloppy, and by extension, so did I. Make sure the person responsible for taking your messages realizes how important a full name is. It is far easier for the telephone receptionist to counter the all too familiar, "He knows me," with a slight laugh and the statement, "I'm sure he does, but I don't."

Along the same lines, instruct the person taking messages to include a phone number with the name, if the call is to be returned. I have been guilty of telling other associate's secretaries, "Oh, he's got my number." The ones who don't take their jobs seriously will accept that. The really good telephone receptionists will counter that statement by saying, "I'm sure he does, but if you'll give it to me again, I'll put in on the message, and he won't have to look it up before he can get back to you." This statement implies accuracy, interest, and most importantly, the fact that by providing the number to accompany the message, the caller will receive a quicker return call. All this "extra" information takes literally seconds to secure, yet the result is a more efficient use of your time, not to mention the attendant savings on toupees and wigs. (You won't be tearing your hair out as often.)

The Crux of the Call

Assuming you know who called and when, the third element of an accurate message is "What did they want?" It is here the exceptional telephone receptionist shines. By skillful questioning of the caller, he or she may discover that someone else can be of assistance. We all have a tendency to take all our problems with a company to the person we know at that company. Here is an example of that tendency.

"Acme Tool. This is Amy. How may I direct your call?"

"Amy, I need to talk to Michael."

"I'm sorry, he's away from his desk. Could I give him a message for you?"

"Ah, yeah. Tell him Jim called, will you, and tell him it's urgent."

"I'll be glad to give him that message. Could I include your last name and telephone number?"

"Oh, he knows me. Just ask him to call me as soon as he gets back to the office."

"I certainly will give him your message. But if I could have your full name and phone number, he'll be able to return your call a lot quicker."

"Oh, sure. Jim Maddox. Ask him to call me at my office. Five five five, sixteen thirty-two."

"I'll give him the message as soon as he returns, Mr. Maddox. Would you like me to jot down what you need from him? That way he could have any information you might need handy when he calls you back."

"Oh, yeah. My shipment's all screwed up. The order and packing slip don't match up."

"Oh, my! Mr. Harrison is in right now. Perhaps he could help you. He's probably who'll end up checking that out, anyway. Would you like me to put your call through to him?"

See how easily that's done? Jim Maddox doesn't really care who fixes his problem, he just wants it fixed, and he wants it fixed "NOW!" Odds are he'll talk to Harrison. And even if he doesn't, when Michael returns, he'll have a leg up on the nature of the problem. If Michael's a true problem resolution manager, he'll have the problem resolved before he gets Maddox on the line, which leads us into the last element of a completed message.

Action!

As stated earlier in this chapter, all phone calls have a purpose, even the annoying ones. If your telephone receptionist has done his or her job correctly, you'll know what action your caller is expecting. The majority of messages will be a request for you to return the call. If that's the case, it should appear on the message form. But some messages are FYI (for your information). A FYI message usually doesn't require a return call. It is simply an attempt to keep you informed about a situation or a particular matter. Here's an example:

"Acme Tool. This is Amy. How may I direct your call?"

"Amy, I need to talk to Michael."

"I'm afraid he's away from his desk right now. May I take a message for him?

"Ah, yeah. Tell him Jim called, will you?"

"I'll be glad to give him that message. Could I include your last name and telephone number?"

"Oh, he knows me. Just tell him I called.

"I certainly will give him your message. But if I could have your full name and phone number, he'll be able to return your call a lot quicker."

"Oh, sure. Jim Maddox. Five five five, sixteen thirty- two."

"I'll give him the message as soon as he returns, Mr. Maddox. Would you like me to jot down what you need from him? That way he could have any information you might need handy when he calls you back."

"Well, he doesn't need to call me back. Just tell him the stock options he asked about are at a pretty low price right now. He can call me if he wants."

"I'll certainly tell him, sir. And thanks for calling."

This call falls into the FYI category. But if Amy didn't get the information about the nature of the call, Michael would probably have returned his broker's call, gotten embroiled in a lengthy conversation, and spent valuable time chatting about something he may or may not have had an interest in.

When Michael returned, he found this message in his box:

> January 2 11:25
>
> Jim Maddox called. Said the options you were interested in are at the right price. He'll be in his office if you want to call him. 555-1632.
>
> Amy

Amy had taken the perfect message. All the elements were there. Date, time, caller's full name, callers phone number, the message, and what action the caller expected from Michael. Michael could take whatever action he wanted. He had enough facts to make an intelligent decision concerning the phone call.

Screening Incoming Calls

It would be nice if all calls could be put through to the intended receiver on the first try. It would be nice, but highly impractical. The truth of the matter is that there are certain calls (and callers) that simply don't warrant the time required to handle them. The art of call screening is one easily mastered, if certain rules and procedures are established and followed.

No one wants to have his or her calls screened. There are times, however, when such action is a necessity. William Faulkner used to tell the story of a time he worked for the post office in a small Mississippi town in the early fifties. On day, in utter frustration while trying to deal with a postal patron, he unwrapped his apron, threw it on the counter and walked off the job. His supervisor told him he couldn't do that. He replied, "I refuse to be at the beck and call of every damn fool with three cents!" How often this echoes the thoughts of millions of us. We wish we weren't at the beck and call of every damn fool with a telephone.

The Invisible Screen

There are ways to screen calls, and there are ways not to. An effective screener does his or her jobs in such a manner that the caller is unaware that a screening process is underway. Remember this: call screening is an obtrusive and rude practice, but it must be done in many circumstances. The purpose of the call screen is to accomplish at least one of three objectives: to prioritize calls, to qualify the caller, or to protect the person called.

Prioritize the Call

Not all calls are intended for the person to whom they are placed. As stated earlier in this chapter, people have a tendency to refer all their problems and questions to someone within the corporate framework with whom they are familiar. To this end, many calls are misdirected at the outset. This has a two-prong effect. First, it places a burden of wasted time on both the caller and the called. Regardless of the relationship that may exist between the two parties, if the person called cannot be of assistance to the caller, then both parties are spinning their wheels.

Second, to put a call through to a person who has no power to rectify a particular situation tends to diminish the authority the person called does have, by making him or her look impotent unnecessarily. Consider for example an advertising client calling his account executive at a radio station. The call may go like this:

"Hanson, this is Keith Richmond."

"Yes, Mr. Richmond. What can I do for you?"

"It's that song your station is playing. The one about insurance salesmen. I hate it! It makes all insurance salesmen look bad. I want you to stop playing it!"

"Well, I've heard the song Mr. Richmond, and yes, you're right. It is awful. But I can't do anything about it. It's the programming director's job to select and play music. You'd have to talk to him if you really object to the song that strongly."

"I don't want to talk to the program director. I want you to do something about it. I spend ten thousand dollars a quarter with you. Now do something about it."

"There really isn't anything I can do about it. It's not within the realm of my control."

"That's a pretty sad state of affairs, if you ask me. I guess you just don't have enough stroke down there. Maybe I should have a different rep handling my account!"

This situation has developed solely because Mr. Richmond and Mr. Hanson know each other, and both are vying for position here. Richmond wants to be taken seriously, and wants his dollar contribution to the organization weighed in the programming decision. Hanson doesn't have the authority to do anything about programming, and is now in the position of having to admit the limit to which he can impact his company's direction.

Could both men have gotten what they want from this situation? Obviously not the way the conversation is set up here. Hanson is going to lose a substantial customer, and Richmond is going to give up what he obviously considered to be a viable tool for getting the message about his insurance company to the public. This whole situation could have been avoided by an invisible screen in the beginning of the conversation.

If the telephone receptionist had taken just a moment to determine the nature of the call, the confrontation between seller and buyer could have been avoided. Let's revisit this call from the onset.

"Good Morning. KRUZ Radio. This is Liz. How may I direct your call?"

"Let me talk to Hanson."

"One moment, I'll see if he's in. May I tell him who's calling?"

"Yeah, tell him it's Keith Richmond."

"Certainly, Mr. Richmond. And may I tell him the nature of your call?"

Stop right here for just a moment. I know this type of screening is not the norm for most businesses. There are several reasons it is not, and all those reasons are bad ones. Unfortunately for most commercial concerns, the person hired to answer the phones is considered the lowest link on the corporate chain. To that end, they are poorly paid, and worse, they are seldom given more than cursory training.

Think about the person who answers your phones now. Is your phone receptionist privy to any corporate policy or is he or she even familiar with your company's mission statement? Do you think of that person as an integral part of your organization? When that person is ill or on vacation, how much consideration is given to his or her replacement? Do you train the temporary person, or do you assume that merely because the replacement can find the phone, he or she can answer it intelligently? In most cases less consideration is paid to the selection and training of the telephone receptionist than the janitorial service.

If the proper care is taken to indoctrinate and orient your phone receptionist the result will be a person who can indeed inquire as to the nature of the call, and at that point refer the caller to the right person. This will result in a much smoother operation, which in turn will translate into fewer irate callers. Let's go back to Mr. Richmond's call.

"Certainly, Mr. Richmond. And may I tell him the nature of your call?"

"Yeah, I'm upset about one of the songs your station is playing."

"Oh. Then you probably want to speak to Mr. Moore. He's our program director. Can I connect you to his office?"

"I don't care who I talk to. I want some action."

"Of course. One moment, and I'll get Mr. Moore for you."

Regardless of the outcome of this call, any animosity that results, will be confined to Richmond and Moore. Hanson is left outside the loop on this one, as well he should be. When Mr. Moore tells Mr. Richmond that programming is set by charts and analysis of data received from record companies, the whole selection process may well become clearer to Richmond. When Moore tells Richmond that in all probability the song to which he objects has a play life of only three or four more days, and that he too thinks it's an awful record, odds are Richmond will cool off, back down, and hang up satisfied. The business relationship between Hanson and Richmond is still intact. The relationship between Richmond and KRUZ has not suffered. Every one wins because the telephone receptionist was informed enough about her company's division of responsibilities to direct the call to the person who could give the right answer at the right time.

Not all companies will see the wisdom in this, and in some cases, investing such authority in the office of the receptionist is not practical. But to the extent that it is a viable option, consideration of such an action is highly advisable.

Qualify the Caller

Qualifying the caller is the most obvious reason to screen a call. The basic motivation *vis-à-vis* call qualifying is to weed out those calls whose intent is not compatible with the ongoing transaction of business within the firm. Many an unhappy customer has launched a one-person crusade to make a company pay for what the customer perceives to be a less-than-diligent response to a problem. This form of payment may well consist of a barrage of phone calls to anyone above the rank of office runner. Moreover, many a salesperson has decided the best way to get a buyer's attention is to call and pitch his product over the phone instead of going through more conventional channels. While telemarketing is an accepted and even desired mode of selling a product, it must work within the framework of certain guidelines. Here again, the screen should be invisible. Let's look at another call.

"Wickers R Us. Jan speaking. How may I direct your call?

"I need to speak to Lynn White, please."

"Certainly. May I tell him who's calling?"

"My name is Linda Johnson."

"Certainly, Ms. Johnson. And may I tell him the nature of your call?"

"Yeah. I sent him a catalog and I wanted to see if he's ready to place an order."

"One moment please; I'll tell him you're on the line."

The option now passes to Lynn White. Armed with the information Jan provides, White can determine if this is a call that must be taken now, or if it is one better taken at a later time, or at all. White will communicate his choice by instructing Jan how to proceed. The purpose of this screen is not to avoid, as much as to qualify the caller. Of course, assuming White is a buyer, he probably will want to talk to Ms. Johnson. But the option should be his, not hers.

The one phrase to avoid when screening calls is to ask the caller, "Who's calling?" Listen:

"Wickers R Us. This is Amy."
"Is Mr. White in?"
"Who's calling?"
"What difference does that make? I asked if he was in."

I hate to admit it, but the caller has a point here. When Johnson called White, she was initiating a call between the two of them, not with a nosy receptionist. With the phrase "Who's calling?" Jan placed herself in the role of interloper. Is Johnson to understand that White takes Jan into his confidence on each incoming call? Is Johnson expected to do the same? Of course not! Then why is Jan asking such a personal question as "Who's calling?"

There is a world of difference between "Who's calling?" and, "May I tell Mr. White who's calling?" One is a demand for information, while the other is an offer to help. In the case of the crisis customer, the very question "Who's calling?" indicates there is a chance the person he or she is calling may not take their call, further alienating the customer from the company. Both questions ask for the same information, but one does it in such a manner as to seem almost solicitious, rather than obtrusive.

Protection for the Called

While protection of the person called is not really a consideration in crisis customer management, it is a reality of business. Most of us have duties and responsibilities that extend well beyond the taking of phone calls. Certainly we realize we must communicate with others, and some of those others may well be represented by an outside phone call. There are times, however, that taking calls is just not possible. Prior commitments, meetings, other phone calls, and even deadlines will force the most open and accessible of us to occasionally resort to having our calls screened.

At this moment, while I'm working on this book, my secretary has instructions not to put any calls through, except those I consider priorities. Certainly, I would take a call from my wife, my mother, or the headmaster of the school my child attends. Just as certainly, if someone calls wanting me to extend my subscription to *The Wall Street Journal,* I would decline to take that call at this time. Why? Not because I'm that important a man, or because I wish to convey the image of a busy individual. The truth is if I am to write a book, I must have time to collect my thoughts and concentrate. To that end, my secretary realizes he must use a degree of discernment in his dealing with my incoming calls.

The one thing he will not do is make any caller feel unimportant or superfluous. He will, however, offer a predetermined response to all calls, (except of course, my wife!). Listen, the phone's ringing:

"Mr. Mahfood's office. James speaking. How may I help you?"

"Is Phillip in?"

"Yes he is, but he cannot take any calls right now. He's asked me to record his calls, and to assure you he'll return your call at the first opportunity."

"Well, could you tell him I'm on the phone? I only need to tell him something, and it'll only take one second."

Stop a bit here. What a trap this caller is laying! If my secretary allows the caller to wait on hold while he conveys the caller's wishes to me, I am then in the position of either having to accept the call, (and I have never, in all my life, ever had a conversation, whether on the phone, in person, or by mental telepathy that lasted only one second!), or I will have to refuse the caller's request. But James is an old hand at this. Let's listen again:

"Well, could you tell him I'm on the phone? I only need to tell him something and it'll only take one second."

"I'm sorry, but he really cannot take any calls at this time. If you will leave him your name and phone number, he will get back to you as soon as possible."

"Tell him Kathy Barker called. 555-2631.

"I'll tell him, Ms. Barker. Will he know what this call is about, or would you like to leave a message?"

"No, he'll know. I just wanted to know if he's coming to the party tonight."

"I'll see he gets your message. Thank you for calling."

Now this is why I pay a secretary. James was able to get the caller's name, phone number, and the gist of the message. And I wasn't disturbed. But notice, there was no subterfuge involved in this call. My secretary didn't try to convince Ms. Barker that I wasn't in the office, or that I was in a meeting, or that I was "indisposed." He told her the plain unvarnished truth. I could not take her call at that time. Moreover, he asked her to "leave him your name and number." By saying this, he was excluding himself as a participant in this episode of "Caller versus Called." He had managed to stay practically invisible. This exchange was clearly between Ms. Barker and myself. Had he said, "Leave me your name and number," he would have involved himself in the call, and thus become a player in the scenario. It is a subtle difference, but one of upmost importance the caller.

Of further note is the fact that he did not say "He'll call you back at once," or "at his earliest convenience." He stated that I'd call back at the "first opportunity." If Ms. Barker had pressed him, he would have told her, "Mr. Mahfood returns all his calls by the end of the day."

By using this method of call screening, no one gets their feelings hurt, the option of when to talk to anyone is always with the person called, and control of a person's time is assured.

There is no way to make call screening totally invisible, but it can be made palatable. The keys are firmness, courtesy, and maintaining a definite routine. At the core of the whole process is training. It is patently unfair to expect your telephone receptionists to intuitively know what your company expects from them without at least a rudimentary amount of training. **Remember this: The first person many people will meet in your company is the person who answers your phone. What impression will your caller form from this first meeting?**

In Parting . . .

The importance of well trained and qualified telephone receptionists cannot be overstated. They are literally the first line of defense for any company, and in many cases, their voice **is** the company! Don't treat your phone personnel as if they are temps or outsiders. Be sure they are soon able to place a name with a particular corporate function, as well as develop a working knowledge of what the general responsibility each department has within the framework of your organization. Nothing can be gained by keeping the first link in the information chain uninformed.

8

Handling Letters of Complaint

Written letters of complaint require different skills and techniques to resolve, yet have many of the common characteristics of all customer relations problems. First, they arise out of a dissatisfaction with a service or a product your company provides. Second, they contain an expectation of resolution. And third, they often strike at the heart of the vendor/customer relationship by demanding a particular type of resolution, as well as a threat or promise of action if their demands are not acted upon.

The same steps normally employed in handling a customer who presents himself to you in person are applicable here. But there are two other steps that should be taken as well. All incoming letters of complaint as well as outgoing letters from your customer problem resolution team should be photocopied. Copies of the letters should be placed in your problem resolution file, as well as distributed to all parties who have a concern with the resolution of the customer's problem.

If a customer took the time to write your company about a problem, it is reasonable to assume that his or her interest in your company is more than a passing one. Inasmuch as documentation is a major motivation behind most incoming letters of complaint, it is foolhardy not to be sure that more then one copy of a complaint exists. Moreover, a photocopy will allow you the luxury of making notations in the margins of the letter, while preserving the original in the event it should ever become necessary to produce it in a court of law.

The Mailman Cometh

There are three reasons why a customer will send a complaint by mail. A written complaint is the beginning of documentation, and often, documentation is the forerunner of a lawsuit. It is for this reason that when you or your company receives a letter of complaint, it should indeed be taken seriously, and steps to correct whatever problem the letter addresses should be initiated at once. This is not to say that a letter of complaint is always a prelude to serious trouble, but as in handling a pistol, you must go on the assumption that the thing is loaded and capable of inflicting great damage.

There are two other reasons, although they constitute a smaller percentage, for a written letter of complaint. There are occasions when actual communication with a company prohibits any other medium of approach. Some companies are just too large to try to iron out a problem by phone, and some are too distant geographically to allow actually walking into their offices or headquarters. Second, there are times when a customer is trying to avoid direct contact because his or her cause is not legitimate. Claims of having a problem are merely a subterfuge to mask another situation, such as inability to pay a bill or lack of desire to fulfill other requirements such as outstanding purchase orders or the delivery of products or services in a timely manner. Let's examine all three types of letters of complaints, beginning with the least problematic, and advancing to a full-blown crisis.

The Little Complaint

One of the best examples of customer problem resolution involving a letter was the handling of a letter my then twelve-year-old daughter wrote to a pet food manufacturing company. My daughter owned a cat. She undertook the care and feeding of this animal, and did so with a great deal of enthusiasm and pride. One particular cat food, of the moist packet variety, seemed to her to be the most nutritious and was therefore her feed of choice for the animal.

Upon bringing a box of this pet food home, she felt there was not enough food in each packet to make a fit meal for her feline friend. This situation prompted her to write a letter to the manufacturers because she felt she had no recourse but to go to them with her complaint. The retail outlet had no input into, nor any real concern about the cat food being sold in their store. And rightly so. If indeed the portions were too small, then clearly the problem rested with the manufacturer.

Certainly it would have been possible for the cat food company to ignore her complaint. She was, after all, just one small girl. The company's reaction to her letter however, has resulted in making her a devoted and steady customer of this particular brand of pet food. This is the very reason why companies engage in customer problem resolution. It is the hope of all companies faced with a crisis customer that they will be able to convert that customer into a disciple for their firm.

While letters of complaint tend to cause the level of anxiety in the seller/buyer relationship to escalate, there are other aspects of written complaints that tend to facilitate the handling of a problem. Letters, while certainly more formal than a phone call or an in-store visit, tend to be easier to shift through and get to the bottom line. If the phone robs the customer complaint resolution officer of her ability to see the complainant, a letter further robs her of his ability to hear and see a customer's level of discontent.

There is an up side to the receipt of a letter of complaint. Most such letters, while stating the nature of the problem do, by necessity, also outline the entire scope of the problem. With a letter in hand, the company has the full picture of the problem, as perceived by the customer. They also know the perimeters of expected action, as well as the customer's opinion of a fair offer of settlement. Let's look at my daughter's letter. For the sake of all concerned, I've changed the name of the pet food company. The cat, however, was named Morris.

December 12, 1986

Acme Pet Foods
10103 Spur 332
Suite 317
Brunswick, New York

Sirs:

I recently purchased a six-packet box of your "Kat Kozy's Kibits" and was very disappointed to find such a small amount of cat food in each packet. My cat is very athletic, and I think the amount of food in one packet is too small to properly feed and nourish Morris, my cat.

I wanted to feed Morris your brand of cat food, because I think it contains all the stuff cats need, but unless you put more food in each packet, I will have to buy another brand.

Thank you,

Valerie Mahfood
Morris' Owner

Now what was the nature of her problem, what were her perimeters of expectation, and what action was she willing to take to see the problem corrected? She obviously felt the quantity of cat food found in each packet was insufficient to nourish her cat. She hoped the company would consider putting more food in each envelope, or at least labeling each packet as being less than adequate for a meal. The most easily understood portion of her letter was what action she was prepared to take if the situation could not be corrected. She would no longer be a customer of Acme Pet Foods.

The customer problem resolver who handled my daughter's letter did an excellent job of satisfying her perceived objections to the quantity of the product in each packet. The letter she received from Acme read as follows:

December 23, 1986

Valerie Mahfood

19451 Troy Place
Coral Springs, FL

Dear Ms. Mahfood:

We are terribly sorry you feel there is not enough "Kat Kozy Kibits" in our cat food packets. We here at Acme Pet Foods know how important your cat is to you, and we also know that you bought our brand of moist packets because you wanted to provide Morris with the best possible nutrition available.

When you bought "Kat Kozy's Kibits," you did just that. Our research has shown us that for most cats, one packet of our food will more than satisfy their needs at mealtime. However, sometimes, someone will have a cat of exceptional physical skills and needs, and for that special cat we suggest you use one and a half packets per meal. The extra half packet you'll have left over will stay fresh in our special foil-lined package until you're ready to feed Morris again.

We hope you were not too inconvenienced by this situation. I've enclosed some coupons you may exchange at your supermarket for five free boxes of "Kat Kozy's Kibits."

Thanks for writing to us, and thanks for trusting "Kat Kozy's Kibits" to take care of Morris.

Respectfully,

Leila Richardson
Acme Pet Foods

This letter may have been the all-time best response letter to any complaint I've ever seen! Let's analyze what made it so great. To begin with, it wasn't a form letter. There was a time when big companies could get away with form letters. That day has passed. Consumers are too sophisticated to be taken in by a micro-ridged computer-generated reply to a common problem. Nothing smacks more of a brush-off than a letter that begins, "Dear Cat Food Consumer," or "Dear Postal Patron." Letters containing such generic salutations are not only counterproductive to our cause, but border on insult.

Second, the letter began by taking a sympathetic approach to the complainant. The company's response did not begin by reproaching the customer for being stupid or for expecting too much from a cat food, but rather took the tact that they were "sorry" she was disappointed. Note they never said she was right or wrong, only that they were sorry for her disappointment. In the same paragraph they praised the complainant for her concern for her cat, as well as her wisdom in selecting their product because it contained "the best possible nutrition available."

It is in the second paragraph, however, that the company shines. You'll notice that at no time does the company ever express any doubt that the consumer isn't right, but they never (and this is important) impugn the integrity of their own product, either. Instead of focusing on the fact that their product is indeed sufficient to satisfy all but the most piggish cats, they point out that my daughter must have an "exceptional" cat, one for whom their product is especially important. Moreover, the letter states that perhaps the solution here is to feed the cat (who they mention by name) an extra half packet per meal, as is the habit of other cat owners who also possess cats of such rare abilities as my daughter's.

Add to this fine letter of mollification the fact that the company had generously sent along the equivalent of five boxes of cat food, and that the letter was personally signed, using a first and last name and what we have here is a case study in customer problem resolution. Every aspect of the complaint was addressed, explained, and resolved. Now if my daughter had chosen to never purchase this brand of cat food again, I would have been surprised. In fact, quite the opposite occurred. From that day to this, when she shops for pet food, the only brand she'll buy is manufactured by the people who took the time to explain their product to a young girl. A quick calculation of the situation would prove out that over the course of the last seven years, Valerie has purchased almost six hundred dollars worth of their product, with no end in sight (she now has two cats). At the cost of about four dollars in time, postage and stationery, I'd say the company made a shrewd investment.

The Medium Complaint

The second motivation for letters of complaint is that the complainant does not have a legitimate case, and therefore cannot stand the scrutiny of personal interaction between himself and the company. Let's look at an example.

March 7, 1993

British Broom Incorporated
13992 West Manchester
London, 3W

Sirs:

With regret I inform you I must cancel purchase order #55823 effective this date. The brooms I ordered have manufacturing defects of such a nature as to render them unusable, and hence, unsalable. I will await your instructions as to when and how you will pick up the existing stock in inventory, and render our firm a credit voucher.

Thank you,

Harry Higgley, Prop.

This letter is a bit more difficult, as it really contains very little information, other than the purchase order number and the nebulous fact that the merchandise provided the seller is of a quality unsuited for resale. When a letter such as this is received, the first inclination might be to get Mr. Higgley on the phone. But consider this: why did Higgley write a letter instead of phoning first? It would seem reasonable that he might have picked up the phone and spoken to the sales rep who handles his account, or at least to someone in the sales department. The fact that he wrote instead of called is indicative that all is not as it should be.

Of course, a letter is better documentation than a phone call, and it may well be standard operating procedure for Higgley's firm to conduct all such matters by mail. If your firm was to receive such a letter, follow your own procedures as outlined in the beginning of this chapter, but proceed a bit cautiously in this matter. Remember, there are several reasons why a customer will write a vendor. The first is to inform the vendor directly of a perceived problem, one not able to be handled with a phone call or a personal visit. The second is to put a vendor on notice that a problem exists of such dimensions that there is no room for mistakes, hence the written instructions, such as "cancel purchase order #55823." And the third, which will be covered in the next section, is to conform to various commercial code laws which require a company to be informed in writing of a situation that will likely result in either civil or criminal legal actions.

Higgley's letter would best be handled with a two-prong approach. Acknowledge the receipt of the letter with a one-paragraph memo-type response. The response should include two elements. The first is confirmation of receipt of the customer's letter, and the second is a brief account of what action is planned. A correct reply to Mr. Higgley's letter would be:

> March 11, 1993
>
> Mr. Harry Higgley
> Higgley's Grot Shop
> 1332 Chestnut Row
> Queensboro, —
>
> Dear Mr. Higgley:
>
> We are in receipt of your March 7th request to cancel your outstanding purchase order Number 55823 for sixteen hundred British Brooms, Model S2. Please be advised Mr. William Davies will contact you shortly concerning the problem with these brooms. We will suspend your order until Mr. Davies has a chance to meet with you concerning the problems you are having with our product. Thank you.
>
> Raymond Jetters
> Vice President, Sales

The reason for such a response is obvious. Inasmuch as Mr. Higgley gave no reason for the cancelation, other than a vague reference to a "manufacturer's defect," it is entirely within the realm of possibilities that his problem with British Brooms are not so much a manufacturing defect as a credit problem, or even a merchandising decision reflecting a possible lower price or better terms being offered by a competitor. At any rate, it is clearly incumbent upon any company to assess the real reason, if any, for the cancelation. If indeed the products are defective, action must be taken to prevent further merchandise from being turned out in a similar state. If the problem is one of the aforementioned reasons, having nothing to do with the quality of the company's products, that must be determined as well.

Determine why the letter was sent, then correct the problem as it really exists.

The Massive Complaint

As previously mentioned, one of the reasons a customer may resort to a letter of complaint is to fulfill legal requirements to establish proper form of notification prior to the filing of a lawsuit. These are the most insidious forms of complaints, because by their very nature there is little hope of an amiable settlement of the dispute. Consider this letter:

January 12, 1993

Wilson Heating and Plumbing
1442 Key Heart Road
Kingston, Nebraska

Mr. Wilson:

On December 21, 1992, your company installed a new XL55 model Trax 90 Super Duper Heating system in my home. I paid for the unit at the time of installation. My check number 1339 in the amount of $1992.33 (Nineteen hundred and ninety-two dollars and thirty-three cents) was paid by my bank to your order on December 26th.

Three days after your work crew installed the unit, (December 24th) I called your company and spoke to Barry Hutchinson, informing him that I smelled something burning in the furnace area. He told me not to worry, and to call back after Christmas if I still detected the smell. It was his opinion that what I was smelling was "new" insulation, and that such a thing is quite common with that particular unit.

On Christmas morning, at 4:26 A.M., the Kingston Volunteer Fire Department responded to a call from my neighbor, Mrs. Keith O'Donnel, that our house was on fire. The fire chief, Richard Keyser, noted in his report that the origin of the fire was the heating unit newly installed by your company. What do you intend to do about this? My home is destroyed, along with all my worldly possessions. My wife is in a state of shock, and cannot function without medication. I cannot conduct my business because of the loss of my home. Please advise me within the next five business days as to the name of your insurance company.

With warmest regards,

William L. Mosely

Whoa! William Mosely is not asking for free cat food samples. This letter of complaint is not one you will want to respond to at all. But your attorney certainly will. It is obvious by the tone and content of this letter that your company is about to be engaged in a major lawsuit, one not only concerned with the reparation of a man's home, but also all his possessions, his wife's mental anguish, as well as his loss of income.

The procedure to handle this letter, however, is not really all that dissimilar to the way the cat food letter was handled, with the exception that all correspondence will be conducted between your attorney and the complainant's insurance company. It is also of the highest priority that you instruct all employees involved in this situation, including the soon to be dismissed Barry Hutchinson who allowed the complainant's call to go unheeded, to refer all questions concerning the incident to you or your company's attorney.

I am not saying to stonewall this individual. I am saying there are reasons one retains an attorney, and this is one of those reasons. In the event you have not retained an attorney, the day you received this letter would be an excellent time to do so. This type of case requires immediate damage control. Procedures must be put in place. You may want to start with a list of all customers who have purchased the Trax unit in question in the last 24 months. Your attorney will want that list, and will advise you as to whether or not you need to issue a recall letter, or a letter requesting the right to inspect the units immediately, at no cost to the consumer, of course.

Your attorney will also advise you of whether or not you will need to bring your distributor and the manufacturer into the picture at this point. Moreover, your attorney will be of immense aid in determining what, if any, offer you should make the complainant at this point. Make no mistake about this. The form and content of this letter is a preamble to a massive lawsuit. There is a time for customer problem resolution, and there is a time to find an attorney.

In Parting . . .

The written complaint carries with it considerable more force than any verbal offering. While the problem resolution officer will be hampered by a lack of verbal and visual aids in determining the extent of the customer's dissatisfaction, there is also an up side to this form of complaint. Written grievances are usually easier to deal with because in the absence of any emotional hysteria, any physical and verbal recriminations, there is an element not possible in confrontational meetings. That element is time. With the customer's complaint in hand, the customer problem resolution officer can take her time, work within the guidelines of her company's policies, and render a resolution which should be both fair and complete.

9

Pulling It All Together

All the procedures in the world will not take the place of common sense and common courtesy when dealing with an irate customer. There are situations that transcend the day-to-day problems this book has tried to prepare you for, and the purpose of this chapter is to bring together all we have discussed, as well as the things you probably already know. Consider this a quick review of everything you have learned over your years of dealing with customers, as well as a handy primer to remind you of some of the things you may have forgotten.

Learning to Listen

It is a virtual impossibility to talk and listen at the same time. This explains why so often after we've been in an argument with someone we have no idea what the other person said, or how we responded. How often has your spouse or co-worker said to you, "I didn't say that!" But you heard them. Didn't you?

When a customer is standing in your store or office and she is raising her voice, it is a natural reaction for you to raise your voice also. Almost without fail, when one party raises her voice, the other will follow suit, only with more amplification. What starts out to be a minor disagreement will ultimately result in a screaming match. This is counterproductive to customer problem resolution.

The next time you find yourself in a confrontational situation, lower your voice. I mean really lower it. Make the other party have to strain to hear you. This will be especially effective if the other person has his own voice ringing in his ears while you are now speaking softly. Just because your customer is screaming is no reason for you to buy into his hysteria. It may be an old saying, but it is true: cooler heads prevail.

Another technique to use when dealing with an unreasonable or loud customer is to ask that person to repeat what he or she had just said. Ask this question quietly, and with sincere candor. Simply ask, "Could you repeat that? I don't think I understand what you're trying to say." Usually, the second time out, your adversary will be calmer, and usually, speak more slowly.

We all try to afford the customer the benefit of the doubt, and well we should. But there is a fine line between anger and abuse. Under no condition should an abusive customer be tolerated or be allowed to continue unchecked in his or her barrage of abuse, particularly if that abuse is manifested in inappropriate language. There is a reason for this. While some people consider it reasonable to allow a person to "vent" his spleen, as it were, the process sometimes will escalate to a physical release of anger, such as an assault or destruction of property. Moreover, the other customers in your store will not enjoy the spectacle of an irate patron screaming at an employee. Such an episode will drive customers from the store, and may prevent their return. So not only are you at risk of losing the angry customer, but you are at risk of losing innocent bystanders.

Try to combat inflammatory statements with gentle, yet firm replies. When the customer says, "You people are a bunch of #@@#$%$# crooks," your reply should not be one of rebuttal, but of conciliation. A good reply would be, "Honestly, sir, no one here would take advantage of a customer. I'm sure we will work this out, if you'll just give me the opportunity."

Notice that the reply wasn't *can* work this out. There is a world of difference between *can* and *will*. The former indicates such an action is possible, but not necessarily the course you will pursue. The latter indicates a foregone conclusion, a faith, if you will, that the entire situation will be resolved. When dealing with an angry customer, semantics is everything. The difference between "What seems to be the problem" and "What's wrong?" is literally the pivot upon which revolves the chances for an amiable resolution. Asking what seems to be the problem is in essence saying to your customer, "What do you, in your overactive, demented, perverted imagination, perceive to be the problem?"

Body Language

Perhaps as important as what a person says is how he or she says it. Be alert to body language, not so much when the customer is talking, but when they are listening to your replies. Are you facing a person with a clenched jaw, arms folded over his or her chest? Not a good sign. If your responses to the customer's statements do not elicit a relaxation of these body language signs, change your tact, as you continue to work toward a reconciliation between them and your company.

Finding an Opening

Try to remain involved, but above the fray. Remember, rarely does the irate customer hold you personally responsible for his problem. Odds are good he's hoping to make an ally out of you, and enlist you in his cause. And well he should try! How much easier the resolution of his problem would be if he had someone on the "inside." This is your ace in the hole. To that end, remain open, and above all, remain nonconfrontational. Observe common rules of courtesy. Address your customer as "sir," or "ma'am." Don't use any diminutive forms of communication. Avoid terms such as "pal," or "buddy." Especially stay away from endearments such as "honey," or "sweetie." These types of familiar references are condescending. If your customer feels you are condescending toward him or her, it is a natural extension that you are also condescending toward his or her complaint.

Every football player and every boxer will tell you the same thing: they spend the entire time they're engaged in their sport looking for an opening. And when that opening appears, they seize it! Like a prize fighter, you need to look for the opening, the window that will appear in every customer resolution process, the chance to solve the problem with a single punch.

When an irate customer is standing before you, defective item in hand, he or she will offer several opportunities to end the discussion. Once you grasp what the problem is, and what action the customer expects, you must determine if the expected action is within the framework of acceptability for your firm. If the two match up, seize the opening. Settle the problem and move on. Do it with dispatch, diplomacy, and dignity.

It is a misconception of some businesspeople that in every transaction there is a winner and a loser. When dealing in the realm of customer problem resolution, it is entirely possible, in fact, it is highly desirable, for both the complainant and the company to win. But to do so will require a steady eye and a sincere desire to accomplish the goal of a satisfied customer.

Looking, Acting, and Being Concerned

We've all had the experience of talking to someone and in the middle of our conversation we realize the person to whom we are speaking has checked out of the conversation. While he may be there physically, his mind is miles away. This realization is not a particularly pleasant one. How much more annoying must it be to have this happen while trying to explain a problem to someone who seems to be in a position to solve it, yet is obviously not paying attention to what you are saying. It doesn't matter why the other party isn't listening, it just matters that she isn't!

If you are in the midst of a customer problem, never give the impression you don't really care. Regardless of how trivial or minor the situation may seem to you, it is clearly of concern to the person lodging the complaint. To afford the complainant less than your full attention is to add the proverbial insult to injury.

Accepting Responsibility

I know very little about automobile repair. I know even less about the electrical system in my car. Recently I had occasion to learn about both. After having my car towed to a garage, I was told the vehicle needed a new electronic module. I paid to have one installed. The next day, while waiting in line at the drive-through bank, the car died again, and again had to be towed to the garage. This time I was told I needed a new distributor. I paid to have it installed. I was less than thrilled when the car required towing the next day, after stalling in traffic. This time, I was not as pleasant as I'd been on my first two visits to my car's dealership. This time, I was steamed.

The young woman who wrote the repair order saw me walking toward her desk, as my now very familiar vehicle was being towed into the work area. I was prepared for a full-scale battle, not with her, but with the person who I was sure was giving orders to repair my car only to the extent that it would last 24 hours before needing repair again. But before I could say a word to this woman, she began talking to me.

"Oh, dear! It's still not fixed?"

"No. It's not. I am not happy!"

"Oh, of course you're not! I wouldn't be either! I feel so bad that this has happened to you. I know how frustrating this must be. You are such a patient man!"

"Well, actually, my patience..."

"No doubt! Well, let me see what I can do to get this fixed right this time. You know, with electrical systems, sometimes things like this happen. I know it looks like we don't know what we're doing, but we will make this right. I promise."

Could I really maintain my anger in the face of this woman's honest attitude? She didn't try to shift the blame to someone else, nor did she trivialize my feelings of frustration. Quite the opposite, she expressed sympathy, even empathy, with my situation. She seemed genuinely concerned over my plight, and in the midst of all the other things she was saying, she managed to convey to me that she had great respect for my ability to handle this problem so calmly. What was I expected to do at this point? It was obvious that to act in any manner other than as a patient, kind man would have seemed inappropriate. This woman had taken my thunder and grounded it nicely.

Mind you, her demeanor was most professional, but she didn't seem cold or uncaring. In fact, her approach to my problem was so personal that I felt I had a friend there, a person who considered my problem to be her problem. She captured the essence of customer problem resolution without any apparent effort. She disarmed my anger, soothed my ruffled feathers, and managed to get me to sign a new work order, without once allowing her training to show. Is that not the mark of a professional?

Avoid One-Word Answers

When my children were younger, and I'd called them on the carpet for a transgression of one sort or another, they would invariably begin a lengthy explanation of why they had done the deed for which they were in trouble. The conversations would begin with my asking, for example, if he or she had broken a particular lamp. The answer I would receive would always include a detailed analysis of how the lamp broke, usually including an explanation of why the dog had firecrackers attached to her tail. After a few moments of this, I would resort to the ultimate parental statement.

"This is a 'yes' or 'no' question. Did you break the lamp?" And again I'd get an explanation that would include the preamble to the Constitution. My point is this: seldom will a single word answer do anything but hurry the judgment. If the child had simply said, "Yes," I would have proceeded to step two, that of drawing and quartering the aforementioned offspring. But by putting "yes" among several hundred other well chosen words, my children could seem to mitigate the offense.

When faced with an irate customer, and her question to you is "Are you telling me that in this entire company, there's not a single person who can correct my account?" avoid one-word answers. Your response should include an explanation of the process required to perform the action the customer is requesting, but at the same time, should assure the customer that indeed, someone can and will correct the problem.

One-word answers tend to move the confrontation to the next level of disagreement, and should be avoided whenever possible. There is a reason why politicians take six sentences to say what could be said in one. Often it's not what we say, but how we say it.

Action versus Reaction

Customer problem resolution boils down to two options. You either act on a customer's complaint, or you react to it. In the game of chess, the player who wins is the one who controls the actions of the other player. The choice is yours. If your option is to react, to follow the lead of the complainant, you will always be one step behind the customer. If you choose to act, that is to take the initiative, to show your customer that his or her well-being is of importance to you, you will ultimately accomplish two things. First, you will establish yourself as a leader, and second, you will help assure your company's survival.

In the appendix section of this book, you'll see how other companies, successful companies, handle customer problem resolution. It is their ability to do just that, to see that their customer's are happy campers, that allow the word "successful" to precede the word, "companies."

In Parting . . .

It isn't enough to act concerned, you must *be* concerned! Customers with problems are not there merely to annoy you, to make your day more difficult, but rather they are there to help you hone your "people" skills. The long and the short of it is that inasmuch as customer problem resolution is a fact of life, shouldn't you be as prepared to handle these problems as you are to handle the other aspects of running a business?

Epilogue

The Chinese symbol for crisis represents danger plus opportunity. In Greek, the word means a time for decision. Perhaps we should consider these two definitions when we think of a crisis customer. There is a clear and present danger involved whenever we deal with any unhappy or dissatisfied customer, that customer will go away from our store and never return. There is also the very real probability that same customer will spend a certain amount of time and energy telling his circle of friends, business associates, and relatives about the shoddy service he or she received at the hands of your employees.

Now it doesn't matter if the customer is wrong or right, nor does it matter if the store is blameless or guilty. What matters is the perception the customer in question has of your store. Perception is reality. Remember this always. If your customer's perception of your establishment is one of an uncaring, money grubbing enterprise, he or she will filter that perception through every dealing he or she has with your company. It doesn't matter how reasonable or unreasonable the compliant is. In the final analysis, perception is reality!

There is precious little we can do about many of the hazards that befall us as business people. We have limited control over the quality of the products we sell, or the services we provide. We have even less control over the way the end consumer uses or misuses our products. We are restrained and restricted by a variety of entities, not the least of which are governmental interferences, vendor apathy and advertising hyperbole. There is one facet of our business facade that we can control, and that is the perception our customers have of us and our company. We can control it, because we are the ones who shape and send out the signal to the customer, of our concern over their problems, or lack thereof. It is the hope of this author that having read this book, you are now in a better position to take positive actions to not only remedy complaints, but to stop potential problems before they occur. It is infinitely easier to prevent a problem than the cure one.

One final thought in regard to the crisis customer. It is not always someone else who has a problem, someone else who cannot find satisfaction in the midst of a dispute. It can as easily happen to us as it does to them. From that perspective, try to consider what it would take to make you whole again if you found yourself on the other side of the counter, trying to explain the nature of your disappointment to a company representative. Complaining isn't easy and it's seldom pleasant. Compound the natural flow of adrenaline in the customer's blood with additional chemicals the brain releases in times of stress, and the potential for a simple problem to be blown out of perspective is exceedingly high. Keep a cool head, a calm tongue, and an open mind. After all, the customer is already mad enough for both of you. The party who maintains his composure is the party that will emerge the victor in any customer/vendor dispute.

Now, get out there and settle the dust, settle the problem, and settle the customer. Turn this dangerous situation into one of opportunity. Remember, no one is more fervent for a cause than the recent convert. Just as missionaries like to use converts to prove the validity of their particular message, you should strive to use the crisis customer as a strength rather than a distraction. Remember: Perception is reality!

A

Stansell Communications Dallas, Texas

Few businesses are as customer sensitive as those dealing with broadcasting. Broadcasters have two distinctive classes of customers. They have, of course, their listening or viewing audience, and they must balance the concerns of these people against the needs and desires of the other group they deal with, commercial sponsors. Unfortunately, the goals of one group doesn't necessarily correspond with the expectations of the other.

Stansell Communications owns a group of radio stations comprised of both AM and FM stations. Moreover, the formats of the stations range from Adult Contemporary on the FM side to News/Talk on the AM side. There are problems peculiar to each format, but the underlying customer service problems are basically the same. To study the problem resolution process for a broadcasting firm, we need first to understand the division of responsibility found in most radio/television stations.

Sales versus Programming

Broadcasting breaks into two branches within every company. The responsibility for generating revenue usually falls on the sales department. Producing a saleable product, on the other hand, is usually the function of the programming department. These departments have separate functions and at times will even seem to be at odds with each another. Programming will often resent the intrusion of the sales department and view sales as the entity possessed of the least understanding of the artistic process. Sales, on the other hand, often regards programming as prima donnas dedicated to the ruination of the station's commercial objectives.

While these attitudes tend to occasionally cause problems between the two departments, the real sticky wicket is that these two divisions have completely different customers to please. Sales obviously must make their commercial advertisers happy, while Programming is primarily concerned with the well-being of the listening or viewing audience. But the one overriding factor of corporate survival tends to work to keep the entire company focused on the main objective: Staying alive!

Because of this dichotomy of interests, customer relations tend to gather into two main areas. Sales has the job of selling advertising; consequently, most complaints they deal with revolve around the effectiveness and scheduling of the advertising copy. Programming is responsible for seeing that people tune in a particular station, and stay tuned in; consequently, most of their complaints are entertainment related.

Let's look at the problem resolution process for a typical radio station. Stansell Communications maintains a talk radio format in a mid-size market in eastern Texas. Their chain of command looks like this:

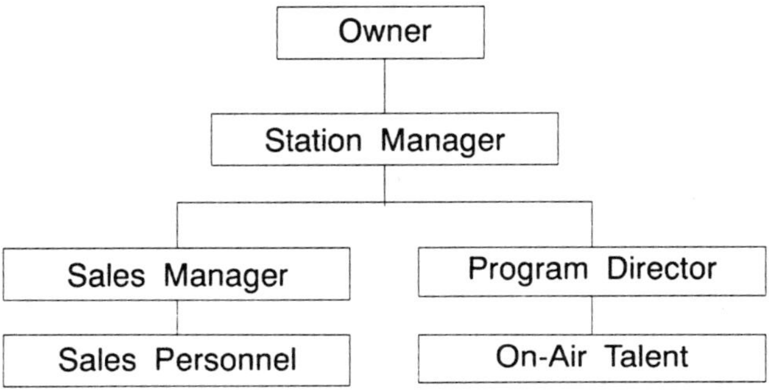

There is a clear division of responsibility between the two branches. Yet problems caused by one branch will certainly bleed over to the other. Let's study the sales department first.

The single most common complaint heard by advertising sales organizations is simply "it didn't work." This is especially heard when the time comes to make payment for advertising already purchased and run. The regular chain of complaints in this case begins with the salesperson who is told by the customer that he or she is dissatisfied with a purchase. The salesperson will relay this information to his or her sales manager, who will in turn alert the general manager that a problem is in the making. The owner of the company may or may not ever be involved in this loop, depending on the severity of the problem and the amount of money involved.

This problem nags the broadcasting industry. Stansell Communications, however, has found a way to short-circut the process, and in many cases, head off potential problems. With each statement mailed to its customers, they include a simple questionnaire aimed at determining the level of satisfaction their customers are enjoying. If a problem exists, this questionnaire is the first step toward its resolution. The questionnaire asks only three questions:

1. Are you satisfied with your advertising efforts?
2. Is there an area of concern for which you would like to speak to someone in management?
3. Do you have any additional comments?

This type of probing, strategically implemented during the billing process, indicates to the customer two major points. First, the company is concerned with their customer's well-being. If that were not true, they would not ask questions one and three. Secondly, the company is ready to address any problems, and address them at the highest level of authority!

This is problem prevention at its best. Instead of waiting for a customer to complain, or worse yet, not complain and take their business elsewhere, Stansell Communications takes the offensive. If there is a problem, or the potential for a problem, this questionnaire will in all probability head if off at the pass.

If a questionnaire is returned with the notation that the customer does indeed have a problem, then the problem resolution team goes into action. First, the customer will receive a phone call from either the sales manager, or the general manager of the station. This preliminary call is to determine the nature of the complaint, and the possible solutions that customer might have in mind. For example:

"Mr. Wiggins? This is Jim Wallace. I'm station manager of KTYL. I noticed you returned one of our questionnaires with the notation that you are not a happy camper. What's wrong?"

"Yeah, Mr. Wallace. My problem is that when I was sold this advertising package, the salesman, Gary, told me that very few of the spots would run between midnight and six A.M. Well, from this statement you guys sent, I counted nine commercials in that time slot."

"I see. Well, let me get hold of Gary, and either he or I will call you back before three o'clock today. Will that be all right?"

The call is terminated at this point. What did Wallace accomplish? For starters, he established the fact that he was the station manager. That tends to impress people. It shows a real interest in the well-being of the customer, one that usually is not exhibited unless the customer insists on talking to a higher level of authority. Amazingly, most companies tend to try to settle as many disputes on as low a level as possible. While this does indeed cut down on demands placed on middle-level or top-level executives, it also implies an attitude of unwillingness on the part of the real movers and shakers of a company to become involved with the problems of the lowly customer.

Second, Wallace asked Wiggins a direct question. "What's wrong?" This question is the crux of the all customer relations problems. What's wrong? Simple to ask, yet most employees avoid that question like death itself! It must be asked before the problem can be resolved. No doctor would rush to write a prescription before first finding out where his or her patient hurts. The same can be said for problem resolution. When Wallace asked, "What's wrong?" he was in effect asking, "Where does it hurt?"

Third, Wallace didn't engage in a shoot-from-the-hip solution. When Wiggins told him the schedule was run wrong, he didn't rise to defend what the station had done, nor did he engage Wiggins in verbal sparing. He listened, without judgment, as Wiggins explained his problem. By not going on the defensive he was able to keep Wiggins off the offensive.

Fourth, Wallace told Wiggins that he'd investigate the problem, consult with the salesman involved, and that either he or the salesman would get back to Wiggins by three o'clock.

This is perhaps the most important aspect of the entire call. Wallace hasn't promised to resolve the problem, or even conceded that a real problem exists. But he has promised a definite time by which the problem resolution process would be underway. Wiggins knew that by three o'clock that afternoon someone would be communicating with him.

Listeners as Customers

Often audiences are not considered customers, but rather merely a group of people coming together for the common purpose of being entertained. But audiences are comprised of individual listeners, each bringing to the party his or her own sense of values, morality and mores. In a very real sense they are indeed customers, and as such, they will take their commodity, that is, their listening time, to another station if they perceive that their input is superfluous.

These people, while for the most part passive in their participation, feel a kinship to "their" station. To this end, many listeners and viewers of radio and television stations will indeed call or write a station if and when they feel their moral integrity is at risk.

Stansell Communications, partly because of the audience they serve, and partly because of the nature of News/Talk programming, is very open to their audience vis a vis listener input. Jim Stansell, the President and majority stockholder of the company, has taken the responsibility of personally setting the tone for customer problem resolution. This is often the case in a small, closely held corporation. Stansell, however, carries this philosophy a point further than most. Whenever he receives a letter from a listener, regardless of how reasonable or unreasonable the complainant may seem, Stansell will either dictate a personal reply, or phone the disgruntled writer personally.

How effective has this been? Stansell Communications, less than 10 years old, is already a dominate broadcaster in two different markets in Texas.

B

Berg-Moran Construction Portland, Oregon

Few things are more personal to us then our homes. When we need something remodeled or added, the choice of contractor is a very important decision. To make that choice most people rely on referrals, that is, testimonials from our friends and family concerning a particular company or craftsman whose work has already been tested and found to be sound.

Berg-Moran Construction is a small business located in Portland, Oregon. They are involved in remodeling and various types of construction work, some of which they do themselves, some of which they farm out to subcontractors. The company, established in 1988, has gross sales of less than five million per year. Their advertising proudly displays their motto, "Customer Satisfaction Has Always Been Our First Priority."

Most of their customer service problems revolve around a difference of opinion about how a finished product looks. Because of the nature of their industry, both the principles of the business are often out of the office when problems arise. Janette Walsh, secretary-treasurer of the company, handles all incoming complaints. Because her primary function is running the office, she is not in a position to be aware of the various nuances of the construction trade. When an irate customer calls, however, Ms. Walsh immediately takes all information relevant to the problem.

At this point, Ms. Walsh assumes a sympathetic attitude, assuring the customer the situation will be put right. It is the company's position that while mistakes will be made, the customer will ultimately be made whole again. She locates one of the job supervisors, who in turn will often contact the customer by mobile phone while en route to the site of the problem.

How far will Berg-Moran go to satisfy a customer? Ms. Walsh said that if push came to shove, the company would offer a complete refund rather than have an unhappy customer!

While they do not employ a formal problem resolution system, they do track incoming merchandise and are aware of suppliers who habitually provide them with defective or problematic merchandise, and have little compunction about changing suppliers if a problem over quality should arise.

Many problems customers perceive to be major are in reality only minor details. Berg-Moran, however, realizes that regardless of how minor a problem is, to the customer that problem becomes the focus of his or her life. This realization relates directly to the fact that the company is painfully aware of the damage that can befall them if disgruntled customers begin a word-of-mouth campaign against the company.

Because some of the work they contract is in turned subcontracted, Berg-Moran takes extra care to be certain that all work is completed on time and to the contract's specifications. Moreover, the involvement of craftsmen outside of their own company places a secondary responsibility on the company to be certain that all materials and parts are of first quality, and that all installations are done according to the contract. As Ms. Walsh pointed out, the ultimate party the customer looks to for satisfaction is Berg-Moran. No one wants to hear about why a job isn't done right. Nor do they want to hear about the problems Berg-Moran has in finding quality workers. The only thing that concerns the customer is how the job ultimately looks and functions.

Berg-Moran stands behind all the work contracted by their firm, regardless of whether or not they actually do the job or if they subcontract. Their customers do not expect, nor will they accept, anything less.

C

Danka Business Systems Detroit, Michigan

Danka Business Systems is one of the largest suppliers of Canon products in Michigan. They are the marketing entity of their parent company, Danka Industries, Incorporated. Their customer list ranges from corporations the size of General Motors down to home office workers. Their field of expertise is the sale and service of office machine equipment, items such as copiers, fax machines, micro-graphic and computer printers, both conventional and color.

While the sale of this equipment is an important function of their organization, over half of their employees are involved in the service of the products they sell. In short, service is what they are about. Because of the technical nature of the product, customers must consider the service department to be part and parcel of their purchase.

The single most common problem facing the sales and administrative departments of Danka is when a machine purchased from them fails to perform to the expectations of their customer. There are two reasons this occurs. First, due to the very nature of technology the users of their machines are often not skilled in their operation. Second, the machines are often expected to perform duties or maintain a workload in excess of that for which they were designed. Danka has developed remedies for both problems.

When Danka sells a business machine to any company, built into the cost of the unit is a comprehensive training session that should familiarize all employees working with these units with the various functions and designs of that unit. This is the single most important step in orientation *vis-à-vis* the operation and maintenance of the new unit. Unfortunately, problems arise when new or temporary workers are suddenly in contact with equipment for which they have received no training. To correct this problem, Danka Business Systems relies heavily on retraining, as well as on follow-up service calls by both sales and service representatives.

The first problem, misuse of equipment, is a bit trickier to anticipate. Misuse is often not as much a case of intentional actions, as it is a tendency to expect newer equipment to perform at a greater level of activity than was anticipated when the machine was purchased. This situation is usually the result of increased usage brought about by the fact that the "new" copier is much more technologically advanced than the "old" machine was. The old machine was producing a given number of copies, the quantity the salesman was told would be needed when the buyer placed the order. The reality of the situation, however, is that the newer machine finds favor within the organization for a variety of reasons, perhaps because of its speed, greater paper capacity, sorting abilities, etc., and now becomes the darling of the entire floor, not just the office or department for which it was purchased.

As a result of this popularity, a machine that was purchased to produce three thousand copies per month is now called on to produce six thousand or more copies. The buyer, when placing the order, could not have anticipated this increased usage, nor could the salesperson. The fact remains, however, that under a work load heavier than that for which the machine was designed to function, breakdowns will occur.

The perception is then fostered that the machine is at fault, and that the company was sold a unit less functional than they had anticipated.

Danka Business Systems anticipates this problem, and has established a series of steps that greatly reduces its frequency. When a machine is sold and installed in any location, Danka requires its salespeople to make follow-up calls, both by phone and in person, to be sure the customer is satisfied with his or her purchase. There is a dual function involved in this follow-up procedure. Obviously, it affords the salesperson an opportunity to follow up the sales call with a customer relations call, but just as importantly, it gives Danka Business Systems the opportunity to be sure any questions the new owners of the machines may have can be answered in such a timely manner as to avoid the cost and time of correcting a problem after it arises.

In addition to follow-up calls by the sales department, Danka Business Systems also schedules regular visits by their service representatives, a practice that also promotes preventive maintenance, rather than crisis maintenance. To this end, each Danka Business Systems sales and service employee receives regular training sessions, many of which are conducted at the parent company's offices in Florida. These training seminars always include training in customer relations.

Inclusive in customer relations training is a segment detailing to the sales department the need to profile the customer, that is, to qualify his or her needs, before the actual sales presentation is made. In preparing the sales presentation, the salesperson is aware not only of the current needs of the customer, but is also trained to anticipate what needs the customer will have in the immediate future, and to include these anticipated needs in the selection and recommendation of equipment. All this preparation results in a better marriage between the customer and his or her office machines.

Danka Business Systems does not stop here, however. Because the businessess of their customers rely on the constant flow and stream of paperwork, a machine that fails to function results in problems geometrically disproportionate to the actual inconvenience of having the copier "down." To that end, Danka Business Systems advertises that they will have a service representative to the site of a machine failure within four hours after being notified of failure.

If repairs cannot be effected on site (and this is rarely the case), Danka will install a "loaner" until the customer's unit is repaired. They also offer what they term the "Peace of Mind Guarantee." This warranty states that in the event that a customer is unhappy with any purchase, he or she may return it for a full refund to be applied to any other machine of equal or greater value. Beyond that, Danka makes one more statement of their intent to insure customer satisfaction: They guarantee that as long as their customer owns a machine purchased from them, the customer will be happy with the purchase.

In addition to the pledge of quick service response time, Danka Business Systems has made it extremely easy for a customer to reach the service departments. Each customer is given the number of a direct service line, a number which bypasses the main switchboard and connects the customer directly to a service representative. A call to that number will be answered by a service dispatcher, whose only function is to see that the customer and the service technician are quickly connected with one another.

While going through employment orientation, all new employees are told that they are the second most important asset Danka has. The most important asset is the customer. Interestingly, almost 60 percent of all purchases made from Danka Business Systems are made by people who are already customers. This speaks to the heart of customer relations. It is much easier to keep a customer than to make a new one from scratch!

Finally, the focus of service is clearly seen in Danka's policy of requiring their salespeople stay in monthly contact with their customers. This may seem excessive at first blush, but this contact has a twofold purpose. Not only is the customer in a position to tell the salesperson whether or not it is operating as expected, but the monthly contact also allow the salesperson to keep an ear open for new sales opportunities, both to the established customer and to new leads that may develop as a result of the customer's friends and acquaintances having been exposed to the products Danka sells.

Danka's philosophy is simply an acknowledgment that word-of-mouth is the best advertising money can't buy! They have made a science out of customer relations, which may well explain why in Detroit, Danka's operation has gone from tenth place in the market to second place in less than three years.

D

J C Penney Company, Inc.
Dallas, Texas

In an age when so many department stores are losing ground to the discount giants as well as the small specialty outlets, J C Penney stands out as the exception to the rule. Established in 1903, J C Penney has seen the full spectrum of the retail revolution, and by anyone's standards, has come out a survivor.

J C Penney's customer relations is a study in what to do right. Their approach to the crisis customer is simply, "Make the Customer Happy!" To that end, Penney's has established a policy on customer merchandise returns that would on the surface seem almost too liberal. If you are a retail customer, you would be hard pressed to have any reason to be mad at J C Penney.

J C Penney's policy on merchandise returns is simply, "Bring it in!" No receipt is required, no proof of purchase, no tags even identifying the product as having ever belonged to J C Penney. Inasmuch as 60 percent of what they sell is in fact "house" brands, a goodly portion of what they sell is easily identifiable. The problems most companies face, that of selling merchandise in common with many other retailers, is partially removed in this manner. But the other 40 percent, the national name brands that could be purchased in any one of a hundred different outlets, are where most other companies go awry.

J C Penney maintains that if the customer said he or she purchased an item from them, that settles the question. Unlike many retail stores, J C Penney doesn't maintain a "return" department. Instead of one central area in the store for the return of merchandise, they have opted to make every cash register a refund center. Most times, however, the customer will return the unsuitable article to the department in which it was purchased. Men's wear is returned to men's wear, women's dresses to women's dresses.

Giving autonomy to the individual departments in matters such as refunds makes good sense. Since it is the policy of the store to make complete refunds anyway, it logically follows that the people best equipped to refund merchandise are those working in the particular department from which the merchandise was purchased.

J C Penney has crossed the barrier from a small town department store to an urban-oriented up-scale merchandising giant. They have been successful for a number of reasons, but a good deal of their success must be attributed to the attitudes and levels of competency displayed by their employees. Emphasis is put on training their salespeople, as well as their supervisory personnel to maintain a high level of professionalism in their dealings with the general public. The whole concept of J C Penney is one of customer satisfaction. What started out as one small store in a western mining town has grown to the fourth largest retailer in the United States.

E

Six Flags Over Texas Arlington, Texas

To see a textbook example of 100 percent absolutely perfect customer relations, one needs only to study the operation of the oldest theme park in the United States. Six Flags Over Texas first opened their doors to the vacationing public in 1961. As might well be expected, with literally tens of thousands of people visiting their facilities every week, some visitors are going to feel short-changed, either by the inevitable overtaxing of facilities, or the unavoidable problems associated with running a business which operates "in the weather."

As might be expected, the most common complaint Six Flags Over Texas deals with concerns the overcrowding of the park, resulting in long waiting lines for rides. Paid admission into the park gives the guest (all visitors are referred to as guests) unlimited access to all rides, attractions, and activities. On weekends, holidays, and the days before and after a holiday, attendance is at its peak. While this is good for business, it is extremely trying on the nerves of the hosts and hostesses (all employees are referred to as hosts or hostesses).

Six Flags Over Texas knows it cannot avoid complaints. Some theme parks place their complaint section at the back of the facility, out of the way of most visitor's line of vision. The philosophy behind this strategy is basically "out of sight, out of mind." Six Flags Over Texas, however, takes the opposite approach. Their "Guest Relations Center" is located at the main gate entrance. It's there for a reason. Hospitality is taken very seriously at Six Flags Over Texas.

When a visitor enters the Guest Relations Center, he or she is immediately greeted by a concerned host or hostess, one trained in customer relations. The guest is treated with courtesy and respect. To fully understand the depth to which this company is committed to quality service, it's necessary to follow a complaint from beginning to end.

The Complaint

"I've been standing in that damn line to ride the Great Texas Shoot-Out for over an hour and a half! If I'd known that I would spend more than three-fourths of my day standing in line, I'd have never come to this rotten place. I hate this place!" Sounds strong, but this is not an unreasonable reaction to spending 90 minutes in the Texas sun on the fourth of July!

The first thing the host or hostess will do with this complainant is isolate him or her from the other guests in the Guest Relations Center. Rooms are available for this purpose. These rooms contain couches, chairs, and tables, which are painted in calm, muted colors. Everything about these rooms exude calmness. The guest is invited to sit down and fill out a complaint form. While they are doing this, the host or hostess who began the interview stays with the upset guest.

These actions are in line with most complaint resolution activities. But it is here that Six Flags Over Texas begins to separate themselves from most other tourist-related businesses. While the complainant fills out the forms detailing the nature of the complaint, the supervisor over the area targeted by the complainant is summoned to the Guest Relations Center. Six Flags Over Texas believes that this is the primary difference in the way they handle their complaints and the rest of the world handles theirs. By bringing a supervisor into the conflict, they are showing the customer just how serious they are about resolving the issue.

The entry of a supervisor, however, does not tilt the balance of power in the room to the side of management. On the contrary, the host or hostess who initially began the interview process remains sympathetic, even empathizes, with the guest. The supervisor is not there to defend the park, but rather to express the park's regret over the entire incident. He or she does not make excuses, but may offer an explanation. At this point, the correction process takes place.

First and foremost the visitor is made happy again, regardless of what it takes to do that. If the complainant is local, and well over 50 percent of all visitors to Six Flags Over Texas are repeat customers, the park may offer free admission tickets for the customer to use on his or her next visit. In the event the customer lives more than 200 miles from the Park, Six Flags Over Texas will actually refund their money!

The customer is made whole again. He or she has complained, and perhaps rightly so, that they were not given their money's worth. The company accepts that as true, and takes the steps to see that the customer does not feel cheated. Pretty simple stuff. When the visitors leave the Guest Relations Center, they leave feeling important, feeling that their opinions were important to the employees and to the management of the Park.

The form they filled out, detailing why they were unhappy in the first place, is then given to the supervisor, who has a section to fill out also. He or she will make a brief statement as to the nature of the complaint, whether or not it was in their opinion justified, and what course of action they will take to see that the situation is not one of a reoccuring nature. The complaint form is then given to the host or hostess who made initial contact with the complainant. They turn the form over and fill out a section designated for them. Their assessment of the situation will be compared to the supervisor's statement by the public relations manager. Each and every form thus filled out will be reviewed by still two more people: the vice president of the division under which the supervisor works, i.e., vice president of food sales, or vice president of souvenir sales, etc., and finally, the Park president.

These people are serious about customer service.

Before the complaint form leaves the desk of the public relations manager, a letter will be written to the complainant, regardless of whether the complaint has already been resolved. (90 percent of all complaints, however, are resolved before the customer leaves the Guest Relations Center.) These are not form letters, and great care is taken to make sure the recipient knows this. While most of them will begin with the same sentence, "Thank you for calling to our attention...", they rapidly become personal letters, indeed: "The problem you encountered yesterday afternoon with our Big Bend Roller Coaster, and the inconvenience it caused you and your three children..." Nothing is more significant to an injured party than knowing they are being taken seriously. The more personal the letter, the more seriously they feel they are being treated.

This procedure reinforces in the customer's mind how important they are to Six Flags Over Texas.

Six Flags Over Texas realizes complaints cannot be avoided. But that doesn't mean they have to be considered part and parcel of doing business, either. The management of the Park uses complaints as a gauge of employee morale as well as customer satisfaction. Perhaps more than most theme parks, Six Flags Over Texas considers their hosts and hostesses to be an integral part of their operation. When the nature of complaints turns from the actual operation or production of the entertainment aspect of the Park to a critique of the personnel, management realizes that it's time to take extraordianry steps to raise what is usually the very high morale of the employees. To that end, special nights are designated as employee appreciation nights, complete with a private party thrown on the premises, street dancing, and entertainment by management. The purpose of this event is to reenforce in the minds of the workers just how important management considers them to be.

The prevailing attitude of the workers at Six Flags Over Texas is that all visitors are guests, and all guests are to be treated as if they were guests in the employees' homes. Attitude is everything. Management of the Park stress that while the facility may be planted, painted, and ready to go, the employees must be positively inclined toward the guests of the Park or the whole operation will be a dismal failure.

Evidence of the type of encouragement the Park provides for its employees is the maintenance of the "company store." Six Flags Over Texas realizes that most of their summer help are working to provide themselves with the "extras" of life. To that end, the Park provides a store in which only employees may shop. This store handles a diverse range of merchandise, ranging from tennis shoes to boom box stereos, all the things a young person may wish to possess, and sells these items to their workers for cost plus the percentage required to pay for the actual running of the store. The Park does not make money on this endeavor, but rather considers it yet another fringe benefit to show the employee that indeed each one of them is an important part of Six Flags Over Texas.

The process of making each employee feel responsible for the welfare of the Park's visitors must work. It should be noted that Larry Cochran, the president and C.E.O. of Six Flags Over Texas was once a part-time employee, working as a Park host, while attending college in Arlington.

It would be difficult to find any organization the size of Six Flags Over Texas that has made a more perfect marriage out of employee relations and customer service.

F

Wilson Trading Company, San Francisco

Wilson Importing, founded in 1984, is a small import-export firm, with sales under 10 million dollars. Dealing with aftermarket distribution of parts and accessories relating to the home electronic industry, Wilson Trading Company sells to approximately five hundred retail operations throughout the United States and Canada. They sell via telemarketing and direct-mail offers, with virtually no visual or physical contact with their customers. They target small family-operated retail outlets primarily in small towns and rural areas.

The underlying philosophy of Wilson Trading is that inasmuch as they specialize in small-town operations, operations that must by necessity use mail order to purchase their inventory, they have as viable a chance as any other distributor when it comes to selling their wares to a retailer. They realize, however, that to earn a customer's business, they must provide a compelling reason for a retailer in Texas to do business with a firm based in California. They believe the compelling reason for any retailer to place an order with them is simply the fact that they provide rock solid service.

Because Wilson Trading is a mail-order company, the problems confronting them are somewhat different than those that beset a business whose customers come to them or who sends sales representative directly to the customer. Mail-order businesses, more than any other type, must rely on goodwill and trust. The trust involved is a two-way street, however. Just as the customer believes when he or she receives and pays for a shipment that the merchandise is inside the boxes, Wilson Trading must believe that when a customer makes a claim for shortage or defective merchandise that such a claim is valid.

The procedure for placing an order with Wilson Trading is fairly simple. The customer will speak to a service representative, either by use of the incoming WATS number, or be virtue of a sales-generated phone solicitation by the representative directly, at which time the order is given verbally over the phone. Seldom, if ever, is written confirmation involved. This is a most informal way of doing business, and in an age of computer generated paper trails, it is almost a dying mode. But because of this method, the possibility for error is immense, and safeguards are taken to assure the minimal number of customer service problems.

The most common customer complaint is shortages of merchandise. This problem is compounded by the fact that much of what Wilson Trading sells are small parts, often packaged in lots of 100 pieces or more, and usually prepacked in the Orient. The problem of shortages is often not so much a situation of real shortages, but rather a case of mislabeled, or miscounted inventory on the part of both the company and its customers. For example, one of the items the company sells is a coaxial connector, packaged 100 pieces to the bag, and shipped in boxes of 25 bags per carton. This particular items comes in five sizes, and seven different styles, yet a passing visual inspection would not reveal much difference between the 12 different bags. It is a very simple matter for an order puller to confuse the various products. Keep in mind that this is but one item from an inventory list of over three thousand different products.

Wilson Trading has taken a number of steps to eliminate this problem area. Primarily, they now have an inspector who checks each order before the order is packaged. This single step has probably done more to curb this problem than all the other processes combined. After the inspector double checks the order, he or she inserts a signed slip of paper verifying that the order has been checked by that inspector. The management at Wilson Trading feels that this signed document is the key to stopping claims of shortages.

When a shortage is claimed, however, Wilson Trading has in place a procedure to prevent further shortages to the same customer. The customer's account is flagged, and a special computer code printed on the pick sheet alerts both the order picker and the order inspector that this particular customer has filed a shortage claim within the last six months. Special care is then taken to be sure this order is exactly right. If the customer then claims another shortage, the customer problem resolution officer is aware that the order received extra handling, and is in a position to point this out to the customer. The purpose of this is not to suggest that the customer is lying, but rather to indicate that the problem may not be originating at the point of origin, but rather at the point of destination. In fact, Wilson Trading was able to assist one of their customers in the apprehension of an employee who was receiving incoming merchandise, diverting a portion to his own use, and then claiming shortages from the vendor.

The crux of the company's service policy, however, is firm. The customer may not always be right, but he or she is **always** the customer. To that end, Wilson Trading insists on complete customer satisfaction. If a problem exists between the customer and the company, every employee is aware that under no circumstances will that problem be allowed to carry over to the next day. The president of the company, whose home phone number is included on all correspondence, is the head of the customer problem resolution team. It is his responsibility to be certain all problems are resolved to the satisfaction of the customer.

The concept of the owner or president of a concern being personally involved in all customer disputes may seem counterproductive to the overall management of a firm. For a company the size of IBM or Ford Motor Company, that may be true. But when a company relies on the continual goodwill of a small group of customers, as Wilson Trading does, the compelling need to make sure all these people remain happy is evident.

By tracking customers who complain excessively, identifying areas of possible error, and installing safeguards such as additional inspectors and order checkers, Wilson Trading has indeed managed to bring customer problem resolution to a fine science.

Index

A

Advertising
effectiveness of, 4
source of the problem, 55-7

B

Berg-Moran Construction, 145-7
Body Language, 81-2, 129, 131

C

Channel of authority, 18
Cochran, Larry, 162
Complaints
attitudes, 51, 53, 161
journals, 24
letters (see letters)
telephone (see telephone)
urgency of, 13
Customer
complaint survey, 25
education, 57-61
relations, 11
tracking, 165-6
Customer Relations
art of, 3
satisfaction with, 156
science of, 143
Customer Resolution Areas, 27, 158-60

D

Danka Business Systems, 149
Documentation, 114

E

Employee
  education, 61-66
  recognition, 9, 161
  training, 159

H

Henry Lewis Chevrolet, 8
Hook-Up Hot Line ,72
Hospitality Room
  (see customer resolutio area)

J

J C Penney Company, 155-6

L

Letters of Complaint, 113
  acknowledgment of, 122
  tone of, 125

M

Mail Order, 164
Manufacturers' Defects, 5

N

Nature
  of the customer, 43
  of the problem, 41
  of the product, 42
  of the store, 43

P

Paperwork, 20
Perceived Values, 5-6
Personnel
  as problem resolvers, 7
  continuity, 7
  training in general, 10
  training with telephones, 84
Perspectives
  historic, 20
Procedures
  regarding Customer's expectations, 79
  regarding industry standards, 73-5
  regarding regional expectations, 75-6
  regarding telephone answering, 84
  regarding vendors, 76-8
Product Information
  complaint survey, 22-23

Q

Quality Control, 66

R

Radio Broadcasting (see Stansell Communications)
Relationships
  customer/merchant, 3
  vendor/customer, 113, 116
Refunds , 40, 155, 159
Refusal of an Offer, 52
Resolution Reports, 69
  as training tools, 72

as verbal, 70
as written, 70
Returns, 155

S

Sears, 67
Service
as a policy, 10, 71
as a selling tool, 151
Shortages, 165
Six Flags Over Texas, 157-62
Stansell Communications, 137-43

T

Telephone Complaints, 81-3
expectations of, 90
how to answer, 84-7
mechanics of, 89
message taking, 94
prioritize calls, 102-5
problem resolution, 91
qualifying callers, 106-9
screening calls, 101
training in use of, 87-9
urgency of, 89
Triage, 28, 37-9

V

Vendors 66, 71
Voice 128

W

Wallace, Jim, 140-43
Walmart, 66-7
Walsh, Janette, 146
Wilson Trading Company , 163

Other books of interest:

- *The Selling Starts When the Customer Says No,* by Richard Seelye and O. William Moody
- *Teleselling,* by Phillip E. Mahfood

If you are interested in these and other exceptional titles,
please call 1 800-998-4644 to request a catalog.